Even M Ghosts

Isle of Wight Ghosts
Book Seven

Gay Baldwin

visit
www.ghost-island.com
for new stories

ISBN 978-0-952-00627-5

CHAPTERS

Page

1 GHOSTS OF OSBORNE 7
Haunted Hot Spots; The Security Guard's Story; Ghostly Bagpipes; Queen's Ghost?

2 GHOSTS AND TRAINS 13
The Train Passed Through Us; The Haunted Station House; Woman out of Time; The Coachman's Ghost; Racecourse Spectre.

3 GHOSTS OF BEMBRIDGE AND SANDOWN 21
Spirits at the Pilot Boat; The Last of the Witches; Ghost for a Shadow; Slaughter at Wolverton; The Rude Horsemen; Spirits at Sandown Pier.

4 HOSPITAL HAUNTINGS AND GHOSTLY SOLDIERS 33
I want to go home!; Ghostly Nurse; 'Under the Clock'; A Ghost in Pyjamas; Night of the Great Storm; 'Unfortunate Incidents'; Pauper Graves at the Workhouse; Ghostly Knight at Kitbridge; Ghost Riders in the Mist.

5 HAUNTINGS AT VENTNOR AND THE UNDERCLIFF 49
Tragedy in the Fog; Soldier in a Doorway; A Ghost Flushes the Toilet; The Doomed Eurydice; Ghost in a Top Hat; The Enchanted Manor.

6 GHOSTS OF OLD GODSHILL 61
Spirits at the Cask and Taverners; Old Mr Bellamy; Ghostly Presence at The Cottage; The Haunted Bat's Wing; The Church Hill Ghost; Old Tom's Ghost; Lady in Black.

7 SPIRITS OF NEWPORT 73
Lavender and Ghostly Monks; Meals on Wheels Ghost; Hooded Guildhall Ghost; The Walking Dead at County Hall; Mysterious Muslin; Ghost calls 'Time' at the Castle Inn.

8 GHOST SOLDIERS AND HAUNTED FORTS 89
Ghost at Spitbank Fort; Ghostly Soldiers at the Zoo; Ghosts at Golden Hill.

9 SPIRITS OF VENTNOR BOTANIC GARDENS 97
The Hospital Refused to Die; A Dark Entity.

10 GHOSTS OF ARRETON 103
Apparitions at Arreton Manor; Spirit on a Secret Staircase; On Gallows Hill; Phantom Carriage and Four; Ghost on a Motorcycle.

11 BRIGHSTONE'S MANY GHOSTS 113
The Phantom Hay Wain; Old Brighstone Church; The Countryman Ghost; Spirits at the Three Bishops; Ghost of Waytes Court.

12 GHOSTS AT SCHOOL 121
The Phantom King; Old West Street School; Goodnight Doris!; Skeletons and Skulls.

13 A MISCELLANY OF GHOSTS 129
Empty Chair at Barley Mow; Pets at Rest; Shide Shade; Orb at Shide; Vittlefields Ghost; Canteen Road Ghost; Cowes Ghost-Ship; Cowes Puritans; Apse Heath Mystery; Ghost at Prayer; 'I Dreaded the Nights'; Ghost in Slippers; Pavilion Ghost; Lushington Lady.

14 KNIGHTON GORGES.... THE ISLAND'S MOST HAUNTED HOUSE 147
The Phantom Carriage; Secrets of the Past.

INTRODUCTION

In 1977, two local journalists published a small book of ghost stories on the Isle of Wight. It was the first time that tales of ghosts and hauntings there had been collected together and put into print. Some of the stories were part of Island tradition; others were contemporary tales of spirits and the supernatural.

That 68-page book, Ghosts of the Isle of Wight, with its simple black and white cover has been reprinted many times, becoming a local bestseller and a supernatural classic. Ray Anker, my co-author, retired from 'ghost-writing' after the first book, but I have continued to research and write about the spirits of this most haunted island ever since.

Thirty years have passed since we took delivery of the first 1,000 copies of that little black and white book. We published (and paid for it) ourselves, so it was with some trepidation that we took it to the Island's bookshops. We needn't have worried. That first edition sold out in just a month! And it continued to sell. The book was reprinted many times and in 1998 it was revised and re-published as *The Original Ghosts of the Isle of Wight,* taking its place in what has become a series of no fewer than seven Isle of Wight ghost books!

I didn't set out to write this seventh book at all – it was merely intended to be a revision of *More Ghosts,* which was published in 1992 and needed updating. But the stories kept coming; new and intriguing accounts of ghosts and spirits around the Island. To do them justice I decided, almost reluctantly, to publish a seventh book of stories. While most are completely new accounts of hauntings, some of the locations such as Knighton Gorges and Ventnor Botanic Gardens, have featured in earlier books. I include them because, as the title suggests, *even more* stories have come to light there.

To those people who have shared their experiences with me, thank you so much. And to those of you whose stories I haven't used because I ran out of space, don't despair. You can read them on my website: *www.ghostisland.com*

In the thirty years I have been writing about ghosts I find that far from diminishing, interest in the paranormal seems to increase with the years. People today are far more willing to keep an open mind about the possibility that ghosts might and **do** exist. Most of us are fascinated by the supernatural. Sixty percent of people in Britain now believe in ghosts, and your chance of seeing one is estimated at one in ten.

A ghost or spirit can be the life force of someone who has died, but not ceased to exist in this dimension. Often they are spirits or souls of those who have died violently or suddenly. Others are trapped on the earth plane, not accepting they have died; or become lost on their way to the afterlife. Some have such strong ties to the living, or their old life that they won't leave. Their dimension is timeless. If contacted through psychics, these spirits are surprised how long they've been 'dead'.

While investigating sightings, I have occasionally been accompanied by a selection of mediums who, as I hope you will agree, have been able to provide a deeper insight and interesting dimension to these accounts. My thanks go to Adam, Chris, Leslie George and Judith. Leslie George can be contacted on 07971 292071. I would also like to thank Barry Price and Bill Shepard for their help with some of the photographs.

There's often an obvious explanation for a haunting like murder, suicide, a violent or sudden death which keep some spirits earthbound. Their strong emotions, tragedy, despair and conversely tranquillity and happiness, leave an imprint, lingering in the atmosphere like a psychic recording, replayed when conditions are right or someone receptive comes along. Are what we call 'ghosts' simply spirits on a wavelength different to our own? Does our undying mind carry an energy, which, after death, becomes part of the energy pattern of its surroundings?

Do ghosts walk when no one is there to see them or must they draw on our energy to materialise, making us shiver when they're around? When a ghost is seen walking through a 'solid' wall, can we believe our eyes? Perhaps we can, for our solid-seeming world of matter is actually energy vibrating at different wavelengths. When defining matter, Albert Einstein described it as 'congealed light'. Taken to their ultimate, matter and energy are one and the same.

So do ghosts exist, albeit in a dimension or on a wavelength different to our own? I believe that they do. I have, over these 30 years, interviewed many hundreds of people from all walks of life, who have seen, heard, felt, or even smelled ghosts. Some of the strange events and occurrences would be all but impossible to make up. Now I challenge you to read these stories and make up your own mind.

In my sixth book, Most Haunted Island, I included a story about Gatcombe Churchyard, which was given to me by Alice Taylor. Sadly, Alice died in March 2007, aged just 17.
Rest in Peace, Alice.

Prince Albert's Walk at Osborne House

Chapter One

GHOSTS OF OSBORNE

The Isle of Wight was a favourite place for the young Queen Victoria. After she married Prince Albert in 1840, the couple were keen to buy a home at Osborne. 'It is impossible to imagine a prettier spot' she wrote. 'We have a charming beach quite to ourselves – we can walk anywhere without being followed or mobbed.'

The original house was re-built under the personal direction of the Prince as a place where they could enjoy a private family life. His early death in 1861 however, was a shock from which Victoria never recovered. Frantic with grief, she plunged into deepest mourning, becoming a recluse at Osborne where, it is rumoured, she began to dabble in the occult, holding séances at which Albert appeared.

John Brown, her Scottish personal attendant, is said to have been a powerful medium whose great influence over the Queen may well have been due to the fact that he was channelling Prince Albert for her. The Horn Room, with a remarkable collection of antler furniture, bought by Albert in 1846, was the room favoured by the Queen for those séances.

Whether Queen Victoria reached Albert or not, she carried on her daily life as if he was still there. All evidence of his death was suppressed in an elaborate charade to give every appearance that Albert had merely 'left the room'. Not only were the Prince Consort's clothes laid out each evening, but hot water and a clean towel were provided as well.

Certain areas of the 200-room house and its grounds are haunted. Since *Most Haunted Island* was published in 2004, containing an entire chapter about Osborne's spirits, mention of ghosts is no longer forbidden there, and yet more stories have come to light. Visitors who ask about ghosts - and they often do - are no longer told by custodians, 'There are no ghosts here!'

HAUNTED HOT-SPOTS

When medium Adam Hodges visited Osborne in October 2006, he was quickly aware of a number of spirits there. He said, "There are many spirits here at Osborne, but the overwhelming presence is that of Prince Albert himself. He is around and firmly in charge. It's as though he is still trying to control everything. He designed the house, supervised its building, and was involved in running the household. He is fiercely protective of 'his' house and is aware of everything that goes on here. Nothing escapes him and he is determined everything here should be done correctly. His presence is so incredibly strong that it dominates Osborne and its grounds.

"Albert's presence is overpowering in a sense that he was 'king' here in everything but name. He controlled every aspect of life at Osborne; the Queen was utterly dependant on him. When he died, she was lost without him. Victoria's spirit may come and go, but Albert's is such a dominating presence that he literally overlooks every person who buys a ticket to visit 'his' house.

"If someone behaves indecorously or mocks anything at Osborne, there will always be consequences. It may be a slight headache; a sudden cough or a stumble; but something will happen!"

In the Table Decker's room and servery, a Victorian maid, it is said, killed herself in despair when she became pregnant. Here, an atmosphere of melancholy pervades an area at the foot of the stone staircase. One cleaner was so affected by this, and the sensation that she was being watched, that she gave in her notice.

Adam was quickly aware of the spirit of this young woman in a black, or dark-coloured dress with white collar and cuffs. He confirmed that she died of a broken neck after falling down the staircase. However he added, "She did not take her own life. I think that another male servant was responsible. There was an unwanted pregnancy and I think he pushed her down the stairs to her death. I am 100 percent certain that she died at the bottom of the stone staircase."

Another haunted 'hot spot' at Osborne House is on the ground floor near a door known as the Ministers' Entrance. A shadowy, grey figure is seen here, and in 2005, this ghost was actually caught on a security camera. As he walked through the stone basement below this corridor, Adam was aware of a woman's spirit above him.

Up on the top floor near the Royal nurseries, Adam saw the spirit of a small child in a white and blue sailor suit with white socks, running happily up and down the staircase.

"He is about four years of age. He was older when he died, but I believe it is one of the Royal princes and that this was a glimpse of his spirit in a happy time for him."

THE SECURITY GUARD'S STORY

The year that Michael Ballard worked as a security guard at Osborne House was an eventful one, for on several occasions he made the acquaintance of some of the ghosts at Queen Victoria's old home.

Michael who lives at Wootton, worked at Osborne from 2004 to 2005. He recalls, "It is a beautiful place and most of the time I enjoyed my work there, but after the visitors leave, that's when the ghosts stir. I was aware of them in certain parts of the house and grounds. While making my rounds at night, I admit I was apprehensive. We weren't allowed to use torches or lights in case it alerted intruders, so unless there was a bright moon, we walked around in the dark.

"My first experience was at 7.30pm on July 26th. I remember it precisely because it was my mother's birthday and I had just used my mobile to wish her 'Happy Birthday'. I was at Swiss Cottage, which is about half-a-mile from the main house, and because reception was poor, I went on to the first floor balcony to make the call. As I finished, I heard a child giggling and footsteps running on the gravel below. I looked down in surprise, for the house and grounds were closed. The path was empty, but I could track the sound of those footsteps as they ran past me. By this time all the hairs on the back of my neck were standing up and I admit I was scared."

Osborne's Swiss Cottage where the Royal children played

The wooden Swiss Cottage, based on an Austrian Tyrolean design was a playhouse for the Royal children who played purposefully in it, learning carpentry and cooking, tending their gardens and entertaining their parents to tea. Other people including custodians and gardeners have also heard ghostly laughter and footsteps there.

Just before Christmas in 2004, Michael was again patrolling at Swiss Cottage when he heard children's voices singing 'Silent Night'. It was between 8pm and 9pm and for perhaps thirty seconds in the still, cold

Queen Victoria's favourite home. The Royal Apartments are on the right of the picture

night he heard the old carol quite clearly. Michael assumed the sound was coming from a carol concert, until he returned to the control room and mentioned it to another of the guards. "He laughed and told me that over the years other people had heard that ghostly sound there at Christmas time. Those little voices I heard singing so sweetly belonged to ghosts."

Another night, Michael and a colleague were patrolling a basement corridor in the old King Edward VII Convalescent Home for Officers, which closed in 2000. Some parts of the old building were best avoided after dark and staff would make long detours rather than use a certain corridor, known as the 'cross-passage'.

"This night I found the door to the officers' billiard room open, so we went in to look around. As we inspected the room, we heard footsteps in the passage outside. Thinking it was our boss coming to check on us, I popped my head out. The corridor was empty. The footsteps however, continued past me and towards the main house.

"My colleague who had worked at Osborne for several years, wasn't bothered. He shrugged, 'You often hear things in this place. You'll get used it.' He told me he had heard someone playing with a ball upstairs in the nurseries at night. There was a regular thud as it bounced against the floor or wall."

While patrolling the grounds one October night, Michael had a chilling experience near the old walled garden, where the entrance to the original house had been. "I was on my own in the dark having a cigarette at about 2am, when I felt this eerie sensation, as though something dense and cold walked through me. I was freezing for some time afterwards. I shot back to the control room where another guard told me that particular spot was 'well known'. One security chap who saw a ghost there was so frightened that he left and never came back."

Another odd phenomenon at Osborne was the smell of spicy curry mingled with sweat, which Michael occasionally noticed in the Durbar corridor, where portraits of the Queen's Indian servants and subjects stare down.

Patrolling the house and grounds by night, it's easy to imagine ghosts around every corner. Such phantoms usually evaporate in daylight, but whatever sets off the pressure pads in the sitting room next to the Queen's bedroom is more substantial. Alarms on two of the concealed pads, one next to a window, the other by a table, went off regularly, although no intruder or malfunction was ever found. Often a chair was found to have been moved onto the pad. How it got there was a mystery.

GHOSTLY BAGPIPES

Now holiday accommodation, Pavilion Cottage on the Osborne estate is a former cricket pavilion built in the early 1900's for officer cadets at the Royal Naval College. Claire Edge and her family spent a week's holiday there in Spring 2005.

"One evening as we were having tea, we heard the faint sound of music. Opening the front door, we realised it was the sound of bagpipes. The sound seemed to swirl in the wind; it lasted around 25 seconds. We took a stroll to ask the security guards if the place was haunted.

They looked at one another, then solemnly assured us there were no ghosts at Osborne! Although we heard no more music that holiday, my son did hear men's voices talking in the empty sitting room at Pavilion Cottage.

Another evening, while out for an evening walk in the grounds, Claire and her eldest daughter had a strong feeling they were being watched. In an upstairs window overlooking the Italian garden, they had the impression of a ghostly woman in a black gown, standing motionless at the window of the Royal apartments.

THE QUEEN'S GHOST?

On December 20th 2006, Linda Denny and daughter Amy from Niton enjoyed a special guided Victorian Christmas tour of Osborne House. Amy took lots of photographs with her new camera. Looking at them on the computer, they noticed in one picture a "little black blob" on the empty terrace. Zooming in they saw it was the figure of a woman in black; her hand visible on the stone parapet.

Is this the ghost of Queen Victoria on the terrace outside the Royal Apartments?

"It made me go cold because it looked like Queen Victoria in her black mourning clothes with a white veil at the back of her head. Another photograph taken moments earlier shows the terrace (closed to the public that day) was empty," said Linda.

Visit Osborne House at: *www.english-heritage.org.uk*

Chapter Two

GHOSTS AND TRAINS

THE TRAIN PASSED THROUGH US

Martyn Smythe, then a young teenager, and a friend were walking along the old railway trackbed which has since been transformed into the Newport-Wootton cycleway. The pair were making their way slowly towards Wootton at about 3pm that warm summer's afternoon in June in the mid-1990s.

Martyn continues, "As we approached what used to be the old station house, where another friend of mine lived (it's called Queen Victoria's Station), we began to hear a distant mechanical noise coming from the direction of Wootton. As we strained our eyes down the tunnel of trees, the noise travelled rapidly towards us, becoming louder and louder.

"Uncertain what to do, we simply stood still and listened. In a matter of seconds the sound was upon us and it was undeniably the noise of a steam train which, as we stood frozen in the middle of the track, came straight towards us, rapidly passed through us, and continued down the track behind, until there was silence again.

"We felt nothing, no trees stirred; there was no gust of wind, or visible sign of anything untoward; simply the piercing noise of a steam train passing through us.

"I cannot remember what my friend and I did next but we were shaken by the experience. We rarely spoke of the events of that day, I think partly because of our uncertainty as to what had actually occurred. However, I remain convinced of what we heard, even though I am hesitant to believe that we heard the sound of a ghost train that day."

Martyn added, "As a child I often played in the woods near the disused track. Even then I thought it was a spooky place. If I had been alone that day I would have been petrified. We were standing in the centre of the old track facing the oncoming noise. As the sound approached we stood still and kept quiet though we could still hear the distant traffic noise on the main road.

"The sound got louder and louder and louder. As it passed through us there was absolutely no physical sensation, nothing visual, just an auditory phenomenon. The sound faded into the distance as it continued towards Newport."

THE HAUNTED STATION HOUSE

At the old Whippingham station this tale of a ghostly train was not laughed away, for the family who live at the converted house have had some strange experiences since purchasing it in September 2005. As well as hearing steam trains slowing down and stopping outside, they have seen what appears to be smoke or steam drifting down the long-disused platforms and past their windows.

The station house has become a large and comfortable - if somewhat unique - home for Sue and Tony Vickers, their daughter Sarah and her children, Sasha and Sam. "We fell in love with the house the moment we saw it," said Sue. "It is a fantastic and historic place to live, and even if there are a few ghosts here we don't mind, for they were here first."

Shortly after they moved in, Sarah's cousin saw a woman dressed in white standing at the far end of the platform. Thinking it was her sister, Lynda, she called her name. When Lynda appeared from the opposite direction, the figure wearing what appeared to be a Victorian dress with a long white skirt or pinafore apron, disappeared. (It may be significant that the first stationmaster's wife was also called Linda).

On several occasions, Lynda and her sister have glimpsed the ghost of a short, stocky man who stands in a doorway off the kitchen. And a visiting friend who brought Sarah home late one night, was disconcerted to see a ghostly figure standing in the window of her room, 'looking daggers' at him.

Much of the ghostly activity takes place in the area of the house which was once part of the signal box, office and waiting room, now converted into Sue and Tony's bedroom, dressing room and sitting room.

On 23rd November 2005 and again in 2006, the family noticed a strong and very distinct smell in the dressing room, which is also used as a computer room. "We had only been here a few weeks, and at first I thought there was something wrong with the drains, but realised the stench was like an unwashed body with a bad case of B.O." said Sue.

The smell lingered in that room for about half an hour, then vanished – until the same date the following year. This time Sarah noticed it first and called her mother. Sue recognised it instantly as the same unwashed, dirty, odour. Again it filled the small room and by the time it disappeared some 30 minutes later, the whole family had smelled it.

It was here too, that Sarah felt an unseen figure bump into her as she sat at the computer by the open door, chatting to Sue in the sitting room. "It was like someone walked past me and bumped into my chair. I both heard and felt someone bang into me two or three times."

Often in the evening, this door between the two rooms, which has a secure catch, opens on its own. Here in the sitting room, Marjorie Smith, Sue's late mother, glanced across at the window early one evening to see the reflection of a woman wearing old-fashioned clothes and a hat, sitting next to her on the sofa.

Sometimes at night, Sue wakes suddenly with a strong impression of someone watching her from the doorway. This often happened in the first three months after they moved in. "I was aware of a presence, but every time I woke Tony, he muttered, 'There's nothing there. Go back to sleep'. I also hear a dog walking across what sounds like bare floorboards in the (carpeted) sitting room towards our bedroom and the rattle of a chain or perhaps keys. But when I check on our old dog, Buster, he is always fast asleep in his basket in the kitchen.

"Only once have I been frightened in this house," said Sue. "I woke one night and sensed a presence leaning over me in bed. I was digging Tony in the ribs to try to wake him, and sliding down under the

Whippingham station where ghosts are seen and ghost trains still run

Old Whippingham Station closed in September 1953

bedclothes at the same time. I didn't see anything, but the feeling of someone there with me was so strong that I was terrified. Whatever was there, it was too close for comfort. Actually, we have moved the bed several times to see if it makes a difference. Old photographs show the levers in the signal box were on that side of the room where our bed was positioned. I believe the presence I sensed may have been operating those switches and levers in whatever time and space it still exists in."

Odd things happen occasionally, it's just something the family has grown accustomed to. Night after night a picture in the kitchen would fall to the floor, everyday objects, especially keys, have an annoying habit of disappearing; something unseen taps at windows at night; and then there are the trains...

At first, the family thought the sound of steam trains was being carried on the wind from the Isle of Wight Steam Railway at Havenstreet. (Now a tourist attraction, the railway runs for five miles from Wootton to Smallbrook Junction, which is all that remains of 54 miles of railway the Island once boasted) Now they're not so sure.

Occasionally the sound of trains slowing and stopping is heard, and one day, while she was talking on the phone, Sue heard a train and noticed smoke, or steam, drifting down the platform in her garden. Although she could smell nothing, Sue watched the 'smoke' as it wafted down the line towards Wootton and disappeared.

In June 2007, a friend who stayed the night remarked casually the next morning, "I heard a train in the night. It must have been around 1am. Is there a railway nearby now?"

Lying more than a mile from the village itself, Whippingham Station was opened in December 1875 by the Ryde and Newport Railway Company, at the closest point on their line to Osborne House. The two-storey building housed the station master's quarters, booking office, waiting room, ladies' waiting room and toilet, men's toilet, signal box and luggage room. Despite its very isolated location, the station was a grand building, which in its early years mainly served Osborne House, the residence of Queen Victoria. Members of the Court and Government travelled by train to Portsmouth, steamer to Ryde, and then took the train to Whippingham where Royal carriages would collect them.

Queen Victoria herself used the station on February 11th 1888, when she travelled from Whippingham to Ventnor and back for the opening of the Royal National Consumption Hospital. The Royal train left Whippingham at 2.45pm, arriving at Ventnor, via Ryde, at 3.23pm. (The Queen would never permit herself to be conveyed at more than 40 mph). Her train left Ventnor at 4.30pm, arriving back at Whippingham at 5.15pm.

At first, trains would only stop 'on request' and the station master would announce 'Whippingham for Osborne'. Passenger numbers were always low and by the early 1950s had dwindled to a handful a week. The station closed on economic grounds in September 1953, although trains continued to run past the deserted platform on their way from Ryde to Newport and Cowes. The line fell silent in 1966 as Dr Beeching's axe fell, and the last train from Ryde to Newport passed the abandoned station on February 21st.

Whippingham was almost unique in having a station mistress, Emily Merwood, who was appointed in the 1890s. Dressed in a white starched apron over a black dress with a straw boater hat on her head, this indomitable lady was immensely proud of being in sole charge of 'her' station. She acted as signalman, ticket collector, booking clerk, billposter, lamplighter and trimmer, as well as keeping the station clean, tending the flower beds and making sure there was a cheerful fire burning in the waiting rooms in winter.

Emily retired in 1912 at the age of 69, but stayed on at the station house to look after the new stationmaster until her death in 1929. Is it Emily's ghost which was seen sitting in the former waiting room, and does she continue to work those levers in her old signal box when the ghost-trains pass by? Perhaps.

WOMAN OUT OF TIME

Val Leslie frequently walks her dogs along the old railway line and over the years she, too, has had ghostly encounters near the old station. On the first occasion in 2001, Val, who runs a care home at Oakfield Road, East Cowes, was out walking her dogs with two clients, Gwyn and Denise. It was early one autumn morning and the track was very muddy, so Val was surprised when a lady in a smart black suit and white blouse appeared suddenly 'out of nowhere'.

The woman, who came from the Newport direction, also wore smart black shoes and stockings, while her expensively tailored suit had a calf-length skirt. "She looks like she should be in an office," Val remarked. As the woman came closer, Bob, Val's normally placid collie-cross dog pricked up his ears and began to growl. She pulled him away to the side of the path in case he jumped at the stranger with his muddy paws.

"The woman passed within a couple of feet but didn't acknowledge us, although I said

Do ghost trains still run here?

'Morning' as she went past and continued along the track towards Wootton. I commented to Gwyn, 'What a strange woman!' She replied, 'Yes, and she had no face!' I realised she was right. I was bending down to hold Bob as the woman passed, but glancing up, I too had seen a blue grey featureless blur where her face should have been. I spun round and looked back. The woman had vanished. I told Gwyn and Denise to take the dogs to the car while I hurried down the path to see where she had gone. Dressed like that, I thought she had been to the nearby crematorium and was upset. But she had completely disappeared."

The following year Val had another odd experience near the old station. That morning she was with her daughter, Vicky, and the dogs, when an elderly couple, accompanied by an equally elderly terrier, appeared on the track from the Wootton direction. They walked slowly past the lane leading to the main road then turned and went *through* a barbed wire fence and hedge, disappearing in the station garden.

"They appeared very old and decrepit. The woman was short and dumpy; the man tall and thin. They were just doddery old dears, which made it all the more extraordinary when they turned and vanished so quickly. We both peered over the fence to see where they had gone, then walked down the lane and looked into the garden. No one was there."

THE COACHMAN'S GHOST

Not far from old Whippingham Station, on land known as Claybrookes Estate, stood a coach house. Built in 1644, all that remains today is a massive well, some stone foundations and heaps of horseshoes. As the new railway line opened up the countryside in 1875, farm workers' cottages were constructed off Tollgate Lane (now North Fairlee Road) and No 4 Whitehouse was built over those remains.

For over 70 years it has been home to the Wollweber family. Today, Tony and Mary, their sons John and James, Becky, James's wife and their children, all live there. Tony recalled, "When I was a lad, the road was just a narrow lane with very high hedges. At the end of the garden was the railway line, with a signal box at the top of our neighbour's garden. I have lived here since 1944, and from when I was a little lad I've seen the ghost of what looks like the 'Sandeman Port' man around the place. He usually appears on the upstairs landing, where even today, it will suddenly grow icy cold; cold enough to see your breath. The ghost is tall and dressed all in black, with high riding boots, a brimmed hat and cloak or cape; just what a coachman would have worn. He never speaks.

"Other people have seen the figure too. He often appears at around 3am, but at other times we see a dark shadow passing by a window downstairs. Often we just sense a presence. As a child, James wouldn't sleep in the back bedroom, and his sister Julie still refuses to stay in the house alone. When we went away for two weeks we returned home to the strong smell of cigar smoke in Julie's old bedroom. That's something that has happened a number of times over the years."

John, who has lived in the family home all his life, now has his own chalet in the garden - not far from that old well. He, too, is aware of a presence there and over the years has become quite accustomed to living in a haunted house.

"A couple of times a month I wake in the early hours to feel a penetrating coldness in my bedroom. Whenever this happens, my bedroom light won't work (although when I check the bulb it's OK the next morning). Even in the summer when the room is stiflingly hot, that same icy feeling can happen. Sometimes when it wakes me, I feel so cold that I cannot move! I never see anything but I'm aware of a presence.

Small objects like keys are often moved or disappear. They turn up again - often in strange places. I'm used to it by now."

Mary, however, was so uncomfortable with the ghost that she called in a priest to rid the house of its presence. This worked temporarily, but after a few years, the 'Sandeman man' returned to his old haunts.

The ghost is a touch light-fingered and has a particular fancy for gold jewellery, especially earrings, as well as keys and shoes. Tony's collection of silver threepenny and fourpenny pieces is also gradually disappearing, and like the gold jewellery, has never been returned. This apart, their ghost causes few problems for the family.

Another more malevolent presence in the garden is a different matter, however. One night it frightened James so much, that he ran the length of the garden back to the house in a panic. He said, "Sometimes there is an overwhelming and uncomfortable sensation of being watched. Everything is fine during the day, but after dark this changes. It can be OK for months at a time, but then the feeling returns. None of our dogs will go past the well after dark. The old railway line and embankment is at the bottom of the garden. Occasionally we hear a train whistle and the unmistakable sound of a train passing by."

Tony remembers hearing old railwaymen's tales of a fatal accident on that stretch of line many years ago. Is this behind the haunting there?

RACECOURSE SPECTRE

At the eastern end of North Fairlee is a long stretch of road known as the Racecourse. Here over many years, a ghost has startled motorists who report seeing a misty figure move across the road and through the hedge at the Wootton end of the Racecourse. Could this apparition have its origins in one of the most tragic and horrific incidents of the last war?

Just after dawn on May 5th 1942, two cottages nearby suffered a direct hit from German bombers. Living at 1, Point Cottage was the Chiverton family. Six of the eight children there were killed in the raid, including two-year-old twins and a baby of just five weeks. Nearby at 2, Point Cottage, three people lost their lives. In all 13 people were buried in the wreckage of their homes; nine died. It is thought that the long straight road at the Racecourse had been mistaken by the Germans for an airfield runway, with tragic consequences. The cottages were never rebuilt, and little now remains to remind people they were ever there. Except perhaps a ghost ...

Chapter Three

GHOSTS OF BEMBRIDGE AND SANDOWN

SPIRITS AT THE PILOT BOAT

The Isle of Wight's branch of CAMRA, the Campaign for Real Ale, describes it thus: *'One-bar pub that is best known for its exterior, converted to resemble a ship in 1935, hence its name. Thanks to its lively and enthusiastic staff, it is now a thriving community pub with customers giving it a buzz.'* It's a great review, but the inn's high spirits may be due to more than its customers, for the Pilot Boat has a ghost, which helps itself to rum and lager.

Michelle and Nick Jude bought the pub in November 2005, after giving up city finance jobs. Shortly after moving in, the couple noticed odd happenings which, at first, they put down to imagination...

Michelle said, "Right from day one I had the sensation of someone standing behind me, and there have been a number of events within the bar area that have no explanation. Since I'm sceptical of ghosts and the supernatural, I have put these incidents down to 'just strange things that happen' but the number and frequency of them doesn't stack up.

"On our first Christmas here, a local group, the Men of Bembridge, held their annual pub-crawl around the village. As they entered the Pilot Boat, the Morgan Spiced Rum optic behind the bar poured itself a large rum, right in front of many witnesses! It's a very stiff optic and has to be pushed up very hard to release the drink. The ghost also enjoys the odd lager, for staff have seen lager being drawn when no one is touching the taps.

"When the pub was closed for refurbishment in January 2006, we reinstated the old beer cellar beneath the bar (it was previously in the back courtyard). In just under a month, we replaced the original floorboards, stripped the bar and redecorated the entire pub. After we re-opened, we noticed many more odd incidents. Gas in the cellar is frequently turned off when no one has been down there. The real ale spears, which identify the beer kegs in the cellar, are moved onto different ales. I have actually wondered if I was going mad when this happens!" said Michelle.

"Coolers at the bar are turned off during the night - again I am sure

The haunted Pilot Boat Inn at Bembridge

no member of staff has done this. It needs a certain degree of force and can't happen by accident. Sometimes glasses shatter suddenly; knives in the kitchen have fallen from a magnetic strip on the wall and 'landed' in the shape of a cross." Customers and staff remark that they 'feel' someone walking or standing behind them and glimpse a fleeting presence. Qualified chef Nick, who is as sceptical as they come, has seen a shadowy figure walk across the locked and empty kitchen, where sometimes there is the unmistakable aroma of frying bacon. At other times, the kitchen door opens and closes on its own.

Michelle continued, "It may be my imagination but when I bend down in the bar I sometimes feel that water is being dripped on my back! It is usually just three or four drops. Of course, when I try to wipe it off, there's nothing there. On Wednesday mornings, I am up at 7am to clean the beer lines. The pressure system in my cellar regularly fails at this time, but is absolutely fine at all other times. I have called the brewery numerous times to come and check whether there is a fault, but they can find no explanation."

After a brief quiet spell, the pub ghost became active again in 2007. Glasses flew off the shelves; the Guinness tap was singled out for special attention, and was often turned off in the cellar. One customer asked if the pub was haunted, explaining that he had just seen a man's ghost behind the bar. And at night if the bar is quiet, staff see the front door open (inwards) and a few seconds later the side door opens, as if someone has entered and left. One evening this happened no fewer than three times. Michelle said, "We are used to the ghost now and we aren't bothered by these incidents. We usually laugh them off. I suppose I would like to find some explanation and hope that whoever the ghost is, we can tolerate one another and live here together."

In May 2007 a psychic lady, who had never visited the Pilot Boat before, surprised Michelle by announcing that the pub ghost was a smuggler with a liking for rum. She added that he liked to sit and look out to sea from the look-out point in the first floor lounge, and that he moved shoes if they were left on the stairs (which he does).

From the mid-1700s until the late 1800s, the original Pilot Boat Inn was in Pump Lane (known locally as the Drunge) where the village pump once stood. This building was close to the old shoreline and its cellars flooded frequently. The pub moved to Station Road, into what were originally two 16th century cottages. The Pilot Boat's distinctive and much photographed ship's exterior was added in 1935.

Bembridge Station and the little 'crabby-winkle' line.
The Pilot Boat Inn is to the right of the station

Bembridge itself was originally an island, cut off from the Wight mainland by sea at high tide, and a muddy gulf at low tide. Known as 'Within Bridge' this was corrupted to Binbridge and finally Bembridge Island. Until the early 19th century, this island was a sparsely populated settlement of some isolated farmsteads and a collection of fishermen's huts. Access was either by rowboat from St Helens or a long detour by road via the Yarbridge at Brading.

In the reign of Charles II, Brading

Haven extended as far as Brading High Street, and ships lay at anchor near the timbered houses. Over the centuries several attempts were made to reclaim the land. Most ended in disaster and numerous fatalities. It was not until 1878 that the sea was finally conquered at a cost of £420,000 - and the loss of many lives.

The area known as The Point was a haunt of fisherfolk, boatmen, and smugglers. It was here that many a cargo of contraband brandy and tobacco found its way into Bembridge. Penalties were high, but so were the profits. Most of the old houses and cottages had secret hiding places, either for contraband or to hide from press gangs, and at the old Pilot Boat Inn, there was an entrance *through* the chimney into a secret room, which was just large enough for one man.

The coming of the railway to Bembridge in 1882 brought huge changes, transforming it into a popular seaside venue. A building boom followed; the Royal Spithead Hotel opened close to the terminus and the Pilot Boat Inn moved nearer to the station.

Eighty-one years later in 1953, the last train ran from Brading to Bembridge, and the little 'crabby-winkle' line closed for good. The station was demolished in 1970, making way for houses and flats.

THE LAST OF THE WITCHES

Until Brading Haven was finally drained in 1878, Bembridge was difficult to reach. Equally remote was Hill Way, nestling in the shelter of Culver Down, which until the early 1900s was a bustling village in its own right. Here, in a cottage known as "Witch's Cottage" handed down through her family since 1558, once lived Molly Downer known as the 'last of the Isle of Wight witches'.

Molly was the illegitimate child of a clergyman, the Reverend John Barwis of Niton. She was also by repute a 'charmer' and wise woman, but as a leading spirit of the smugglers' gangs, her reputation as a witch may have been somewhat exaggerated to keep superstitious folks away. Neighbours claimed Molly owned dolls into which she would stick pins when someone upset her.

Molly, they whispered had placed a curse on Harriet, a young girl who teased and mocked her. If ever good fortune should befall her, she would not live to enjoy it. Soon afterwards, Harriet was paralysed and died on the very day that she was due to receive a legacy. Molly, too, died in mysterious circumstances. She was found dead on the floor of her locked cottage, carefully laid out with arms folded across her chest. Her neighbours thought that Molly possessed a secret treasure. The clergyman to whom she had willed her cottage, ordered Molly's body to be taken from the coffin and stripped to see if money or anything of value was hidden there. Nothing was found and Molly, the 'last witch of Wight' was reclothed, recoffined and buried in an unmarked grave in Brading churchyard.

GHOST FOR A SHADOW

Not far from Whitecliff Bay is an old stone cottage with thick limestone walls. When it featured in Lloyd Grossman's 'Through the Keyhole' television programme, the presenter acknowledged it as one of his best. Here, surrounded by rock memorabilia; guitars, photographs (from his time as a professional photographer) and souvenirs of his years in the music business, lives former Shadow, Jet Harris.

The Shadows were Britain's most popular group before the Beatles. As backing group for Cliff Richard, and with their own instrumental hits, by 1962, The Shadows enjoyed almost thirty top twenty hits.

Jet and his wife Janet moved into the 15th century cottage off Peacock Hill, Bembridge in 1999. From the moment they set foot in the house they were embraced by its warm, welcoming atmosphere and a sense of acceptance. "I could never move, I love the place too much," said Jet. "When I have been away or on tour, I am always relieved to get back on the ferry and come home."

And home it is, for although he wasn't born on the Island, Jet admits he was conceived here when his parents were on honeymoon! "From 1946 onwards our family spent many happy holidays here. For 50 years, I vowed that one day I would live here. Now I do and the Isle of Wight is a spiritual home for me."

Although the cottage's resident spirit is not bothersome, Jet has told few people about it. "Shortly after we moved in, Janet was aware of 'something' here. She felt it was a child, because its antics are mischievous.

"Before we had our cats, we heard a clattering noise downstairs one day. There, in the middle of the wooden table was a cut glass vase (which had been shut in a cupboard) spinning slowly around. We were puzzled to say the least. Another day we came home from shopping to find the front door mat had been moved from its usual spot and placed at the foot of the stairs. Sitting on top of it were my old slippers.

"Then one day, Janet, who smoked roll-ups, lost her tobacco. She hunted high and low, but the pack of Golden Virginia had vanished. We later found it inside an old sideboard, wedged behind the sofa.

"When I am sitting in the front room I occasionally glimpse 'a shadow' passing by the door. I thought I was imagining it at first, but it has happened a number of times and I'm not the only one to see it. My cat, Diesel, would sometimes sit bolt upright, with eyes like saucers, staring intently for several minutes at that doorway. He was clearly following the movements of something only he

Former Shadow Jet Harris in his haunted cottage at Bembridge

could see. It was unnerving, because his fur bushed up and he was aware of something invisible.

"When I am alone in the cottage, I sometimes hear a voice calling 'Terry, Terry', which is my real name. Things are moved or disappear here; little things like keys or something I am working on. I put them down, turn around and they're gone. Usually they reappear some time later. It's just mischievous and something you get used to in this cottage."

SLAUGHTER AT WOLVERTON

Nearby is the curiously named St Urian's Copse, where French raiders destroyed the vanished settlement of Wolverton in the fourteenth century. The attackers burnt the wooden houses to the ground and those townsfolk who did not escape into the woods were slaughtered. Wolverton had its own well, a navigable channel, harbour and St Urian's Chapel nearby. It's curious therefore that it was abandoned. No doubt superstition played a part, for legend tells that the ruins were cursed. Not only was the place accursed, it was also haunted. People started to avoid the ruins after dark, refusing to venture down Pilgrim Lane where even today the grey ghost of a pilgrim is still said to walk.

Today the village lies underneath St Urian's - or Centurion's - Copse, which each spring is filled with wild daffodils. Excavations there have revealed stone walls, domestic utensils, slate, flint and pottery.

But Wolverton is strangely silent. An atmosphere of menace hangs in the air. If you are brave enough to visit at twilight, stand quietly and listen.

Some folk claim to hear sounds of battle and cries of the murdered townspeople. Since the slaughter, it's said that no nightingale will sing in Wolverton Woods....

THE RUDE HORSEMEN

Freddie Morris had a strange encounter with three ghosts on horseback near Borthwood Copse, one day in 1987. Freddie had just rounded a sharp bend in his car when he saw the horsemen in what looked like fancy dress, riding three abreast in the road ahead.

"Although the horses and riders appeared solid, they made no sound. I recall only one man clearly. He was on the left and wore a three-cornered hat. The other two had grey wigs with small pigtails, tied as I recall with black ribbon. That surprised me as I thought the wigs would be white, but they were a dirty, off-white colour. The clothes were not new, but well worn.

"I thought they were most rude because they took up the whole road. They didn't seem aware of me, or my car, at all. I never overtake horses unless it is safe, so I followed behind them, until they turned onto a bridle path to Newchurch and then vanished.

"As I started to drive home, still fuming about the way they had blocked the road, I realised they were ghosts. I am still wary when I drive through Borthwood Shute, for I half expect to meet them again."

SPIRITS AT SANDOWN PIER

Until the 19th century, Sandown had little to offer visitors. It was nothing more than a fishing village with a Tudor fort and garrison, set in the middle of the five-mile stretch of golden sands of Sandown Bay. It wasn't until John Wilkes, a former Mayor of London and member of the notorious Hell Fire Club, retired to 'Sandham' that it started to grow to become the fashionable watering place for smart society and ultimately the seaside resort of Sandown.

A pier for promenading along was essential. One was built in 1879, but this only extended 360 feet because the Sandown Pier Company ran out of money! In 1895, it was lengthened to 875 feet and a domed pavilion was added. In 1933, Sandown Pier was further extended as a new 1,000-seat pavilion was built at the shoreward end. The original pavilion at the pierhead became a ballroom.

In 1968, a major redevelopment of the entire pier structure started. The pavilion at the seaward end was demolished; many iron piles and much of the wooden decking were replaced. When it re-opened in 1973, the pier boasted a 980-seat theatre, the largest on the Island at the time. Many big stars, including Jimmy Tarbuck, Cilla Black, Lenny Henry and Bob Monkhouse, topped the bill there.

In August 1989, an electrical fault caused a serious fire in the theatre and £2 million worth of damage. The only fatalities were three doves used by illusionist Richard Devere. The building re-opened, but closed for good a decade later to be replaced by Magic Island Playground and the Lost World Indoor Adventure Golf Course.

Even without its theatre, the pier is still a magnet for visitors - and for ghosts too. For manager Colin Baldock, who has worked there since 1991, they are part of life on the pier. Most supernatural activity centres around the old theatre site, where the hazy silhouette of a man walks towards the golf course. Former employee, Jenna Sheath, described a dark cloaked figure walking through a wall. Colin has seen this ghost twice himself.

"Late at night when the place is quiet, it can feel very spooky indeed. Sometimes the smell of old cigarette smoke drifts across the play area, where the theatre's upper auditorium used to be. There have been a number of deaths on the pier, including some in the theatre; perhaps that's why the ghosts linger there," said Colin.

Over a century ago, one young chambermaid threw herself off the pier, killing herself and her unborn child. Once the story became public, her married lover, a respected local man - a lay preacher and organist at the nearby church - drowned himself, too, by walking into the sea beneath the pier.

Sandown Pier and its former haunted theatre is now an entertainment complex

It's not just the ghosts of people haunting the pier. Colin has seen what he believes are the spirits of the doves which perished in their cage in the fire; small fluttering lights, with bright auras, which appeared in that old theatre area.

One night, Colin, his wife, and another employee Malcolm, were working late on the pier. "I asked Malcolm to sweep up because we had had builders in. As he worked I was messing around in the dark, throwing some small bits of wood at him. A short while later I had to go to the far end of the pier. I had my radio with me and as I keyed it, I heard Malcolm talking. He sounded cross as he said, 'It's getting dangerous. Stop throwing that wood. The pieces are too big!'

"I called him up to ask what was going on. He complained that I was still throwing wood at him, and wouldn't believe it wasn't me. I had to put my wife on the radio to convince him that we were at the other end of the pier. None of us stayed there long that night."

Visitors to the amusement arcade also report 'odd' happenings. Louise Braine of Ventnor is among them. She explained, "It was January 2005, and after having a tough week, my husband Alan and I went out for the afternoon with Jake, our four-year-old, to have some fun on Sandown Pier. I started to play on the 2p shuffle machines with Jake,

Sandown Pier and its haunted theatre is pictured here in the 1930s

while Alan went for more change. I felt a sharp yank on the back of my coat and spun around, thinking it was Alan, but there was no one there. In fact there was no one anywhere near me, but I am sure of what I felt. When Alan returned I told him of my experience. He laughed and told me I had been watching too much 'Most Haunted', said Louise"

Now working as manager at Shankin Theatre, Chris Gardner was technical manager at Sandown Theatre from 1987 until it closed in 2000. In June 1991, he was present in the empty theatre when entertainer John Martin and impressionist Marc Duane saw a ghost on stage one night, after the show.

In an interview recorded for the Isle of Wight Radio show 'John Hannam Meets', John Martin said, "I saw a man standing in the middle of the stage, laughing. Then he turned ninety degrees, looked at us, and walked off stage, straight through the curtain. We thought at first it was a joke. Then it dawned on us that it wasn't. I screamed and ran for the security guard. The situation was just so weird. Although he looked at us, it was like we weren't there. The theatre suddenly felt freezing cold, but I began sweating heavily. It wasn't a ghost like you imagine, he looked like a normal solid person. For the first time in my life, I was speechless in a theatre!"

Marc added, "I don't believe in ghosts, but I saw one with my own eyes that night. John was as white as a sheet; I was hysterical. There was no gap in that curtain where the ghost passed through. I checked thoroughly."

Chris added. "There were only three of us in the building. I was upstairs in the office when John and Marc saw the figure standing between the curtain and back canvas. They were so shaken that they ran outside to find the security guard. We checked everywhere but found no one. But of course most theatres are haunted ... Sandown was no exception."

The fashionable seaside resort of Sandown in 1863, pictured before its pier was built

The clock tower at old Whitecroft Hospital looms over the site

Chapter Four

HOSPITAL HAUNTINGS AND GHOSTLY SOLDIERS

Like a small self-contained town, Whitecroft Hospital was an Island institution for a century. This 'Isle of Wight County Lunatic Asylum', which was planned to have a chapel, farm, mortuary, cemetery and 500-ft deep well, opened without ceremony in 1896 at a cost of £45,000 after delays caused by bad weather, strikes and a fever epidemic. Built of 3.5 million red bricks made on site, the hospital could take 380 'inmates' in two-storey blocks or wards, each containing up to 50 patients. Male wards were named after explorers, female wards after poets and writers.

As attitudes to mental health changed, it became Whitecroft Mental Hospital, then Whitecroft Hospital. When it closed in 1990, patients were transferred to the Newcroft unit at St Mary's Hospital, Newport, and later to Sevenacres, a £5.2 million purpose-built unit - 100 times more than Whitecroft cost. Near the main gate at Whitecroft was a separate block built after the main wards. This was the Rhodes/Tennyson ward for private patients and it even boasted its own billiard room.

A century after the first Victorian pauper inmates were admitted, Whitecroft Hospital is no more. Like other redundant asylums elsewhere in the country, it is being redeveloped, converted and reincarnated as 'The Palm' development of 115 luxury houses and apartments set around the clock tower in 25 acres of grounds.

Surrey-based Oakdene Homes proudly announced, *"An eclectic mix of apartments converted from a late Victorian hospital, this landmark project features fabulous architecture with a listed clock tower. The Palm will offer a gated community lifestyle with many facilities. A taste of island life without airport hassle situated in the very heart of the island and wrapped around by rolling countryside. The Palm offers a range of two and three bedroom apartments and three and four bedroom houses with exclusive leisure facilities, including a fitness centre, pool and tennis court, just a short drive from Fishbourne car ferry terminal."*

By 2007 with work underway, the site was protected by 24-hour security to deter vandals, squatters ... and, of course, ghost hunters. For the old hospital has long been reported, documented, and well-known as a most haunted place, with paranormal groups given permission to investigate ghosts there in the past.

Even after the hospital itself closed, office staff complained about occasional but overpowering smells of soiled clothing. (Read about other ghosts at Whitecroft in *Ghosts of the Isle of Wight Book Four*) So, when former retained fireman, Michael Ballard of Wootton, started work as a security guard in 2005, his first posting was nearly his last - after he was sent to the old hospital site.

I WANT TO GO HOME!

Michael explains, "I was taken out there by one of the other guys and shown where to patrol. Then I was left on my own for the rest of the shift. As I walked around, I noticed a horrible smell. Thinking I had stepped in something unpleasant, I checked my shoes. Nothing there. However that smell, like sewage and badly soiled nappies, followed me everywhere. It was vile.

"I went back to the security office in the laundry building from where I could watch the main driveway. Suddenly there was an almighty bang behind me. I spun round to see the blue door leading to the old washing area had slammed shut. I thought to myself, I really don't like it here. I want to go home!

"But I opened the door and checked the room thoroughly. Everything was secure, the place was empty and the windows locked. I shut the door again and locked it. As I did so I heard loud, maniacal laughter. I have never been so frightened in all my life. It was a crazy, insane woman's cackling laugh coming from behind the door I had just locked, from the empty room I had just checked. It continued for several seconds, but seemed like an eternity. I rang my boss and told him I couldn't work at Whitecroft any more. I locked up and left."

Michael did however return a few months later to supervise other staff, and one night, while pulling up in his van, he saw candlelight in a first-floor window in the old private ward. Looking more closely he saw a white forehead reflected in the light. He got back in the van, locked the door, then looked again. The candle and figure had gone. He never told the guard what he'd seen.

GHOSTLY NURSE

Other security guards and builders, past and present, have their own stories to tell. The strong smell of ether is often reported in the old

Staff in the old kitchens at Whitecroft Hospital

private ward; sometimes this is so overpowering it lingers all night long. Here, too, security guards often have a strong sensation that 'someone' is watching them.

A ghostly nurse wheeling an old-fashioned black bicycle has been seen on several occasions. A workman saw, and spoke to her, one Saturday afternoon in 2006. "She was wheeling an old nurses' bike as she came towards me. I asked her what she was doing. She replied that she had worked here and wanted to look around. When I told her the site was private and she would have to leave, she walked away. Then I realised that although she looked solid, the woman who seemed ageless, had been wearing a very old-fashioned nurse's uniform from the 1920s or 30s, with wide red straps crossing her blouse and white apron."

Could this be the same spirit which medium Leslie George sensed when he visited the old hospital some time earlier? This woman named Wendy, wearing a large old-fashioned nurses' hat, was a senior nurse there for 22 years from the 1920s to the 1940s. "She was in her late fifties when she died and she said that she still had work to do at the hospital. Nurse Wendy is very active here, she continues to make her rounds and keeps a close eye on the place," said Les. She is sometimes accompanied by a ghost dog, a little brown mongrel which still walks about the place. He was 'much loved' Wendy told Les.

Whitecroft Hospital's laundry maids at work

In the former nurses' block behind the hospital, doors open and close on their own. Workers on site sometimes feel a ghostly hand tap them on the shoulder; they also complain that tools vanish, or are moved by unseen hands. One of the worst places for this is the base of the clock tower. Some of the men refuse to work there; others just treat it as a laugh.

A misty white figure moves across an old car park near the laundry. This ghost, believed to be a former doctor, stops to peer into one of the empty rooms before vanishing. The figure of a young man in his twenties has also been seen running nearby by several people. Another doctor or senior member of staff has been seen in one of the patient blocks. This smartly-dressed spirit in a dark suit and cravat, with an unkempt mop of hair, moves quickly through the first floor wards, followed by an assistant who hurries along behind.

When the security office was in a caravan next to the old laundry, guards would sometimes hear a terrific banging sound as if a fist was hammering on the door. And sometimes inside the caravan, there would be the smell of smouldering wood as though the place was on fire.

Several times they stripped everything out, but found nothing wrong. One guard, Steve, watched in astonishment as an incandescent ball of white light passed right through the caravan and his car one night. Travelling at walking pace, at waist height, this large orb rippled like a wave as it floated around the perimeter of the building.

After finishing work one night, Steve stopped to unlock the gate outside the old private ward, to drive out into the lane. Once back into his car he noticed a cold draught. While he was out of the car 'someone' had wound down his passenger window.

'UNDER THE CLOCK'

The old clock tower, visible for many miles around, still dominates the site. The clock, with its two faces, is part of the Island life, and the local saying that someone was 'under the clock' was a euphemism for being a patient at Whitecroft. Former site guards Colin and Steve, agree that old clock tower is a strange place.

"Although the clock doesn't work, the hands on one of the faces still move at times. It doesn't happen if you watch, but when you look away, the hour hand will have changed. One night just before 10pm, we were coming back from patrol when we saw a light in the clock tower as though someone with a candle was climbing up inside. As the light moved up the tower we could see the glow coming from each of the windows in turn.

"We ran to check that all the doors and windows were locked. They were. However, as we sat and watched (we could not get into the tower) the light hovered around the top for almost half-an-hour. It wasn't a torch; the light was much softer, like the pale flickering of candlelight."

The ghost nurse was seen with a bicycle near this old ward

The little ghost of a sobbing girl is heard, and occasionally glimpsed around the old hospital. At other times she is seen playing happily with a ball in the grounds. In one of the deserted female wards, perhaps once used for 'lying-in' (the old term for childbirth) a woman's screams have been heard, followed by the wail of a baby.

This strange misty shape appeared on a photograph taken in March 2005

A Misty Shape

Michael Trigg sent me the photograph (shown above) taken at Whitecroft Hospital at 5pm in early March 2005. The interior was light and dust free. The temperature was variable, swinging wildly from warm to sudden cold. This digital picture was taken in the deserted, old private Tennyson/Rhodes ward. No anomalies were visible to the naked eye at the time, Michael reports.

A GHOST IN PYJAMAS

Jo Hendy (not her real name) of Newport spent much of her nursing career at Whitecroft. During her years there, she heard many tales of ghosts and hauntings but it wasn't until she saw one herself that she became a believer.

Jo worked nights on Shackleton Ward, which was originally built for elderly male patients, although latterly it was a mixed ward. "At the end of the shift we woke and washed the patients, changed the sheets and put them back to bed, ready for the day staff. I wheeled the soiled linen down the long corridor to the laundry, past some little curtained cubicles, each containing a washbasin and mirror.

"I glanced into the first cubicle. Standing looking into the mirror was a little old man wearing a long pyjama jacket – and nothing else. I thought to myself, 'Who on earth is that? I have just put them all to bed.' I looked again but he wasn't there!

"It was so vivid that years later, I can still picture him. He must have been in his eighties, slightly built, with very sparse, white hair.

An aerial view of the Whitecroft Hospital site taken shortly before it closed

Fortunately, his pink and beige striped pyjama jacket was quite long, for he wasn't wearing any trousers. He didn't seem aware of me as he stood gazing at the mirror.

"The hairs stood up on the back of my neck. This was a ghost. I was so frightened my heart was racing. I raced down the corridor and when I saw a colleague, I asked her to feel my pulse. When she remarked that it was really fast, I told her that was because I had just seen a ghost!"

NIGHT OF THE GREAT STORM

On the night of the hurricane in October 1987, Mark Earp, who worked in many Island hospitals on maintenance duties, was called in after a roof at Whitecroft was damaged. Rain was threatening the thousands of old medical records from doctors and hospitals all over the Island, which were stored there.

"The records were piled from floor to ceiling in thirty racks, ten feet high and fifty feet long," said Mark. "After my colleague and I managed to get a tarpaulin on the damaged roof, we went into the record room to check that the leaks had stopped. As I stood with the wind howling outside, a single medical record card four rows behind me emerged from the rack and fell to the floor, as though 'something' was trying to attract my attention"

Mark picked it up. Turning the envelope over, he discovered the card was his mother's record. "I was speechless," said Mark. "But Whitecroft was a strange place with some very disturbed energy there. When I worked in the mortuary the atmosphere there was unnaturally cold. At times it would become so chilled that the energy felt like a blast of freezing air."

'UNFORTUNATE INCIDENTS'

Although Whitecroft Hospital was built in relative isolation, there was ongoing conflict with its neighbours. In 1934, in a series of letters headed 'Walking Parties' and 'Wandering Lunatics', Sir Claud Vere Hobart, director of the Langdown Estate Company, Standen House, Newport (who listed his recreations in Who's Who as hunting and big game shooting) wrote to the Medical Superintendent complaining about the 'lax system of control' and the annoyance caused by parties of male and female inmates being sent out on the roads and lanes causing nuisance and terror in the neighbourhood.

He wrote in one letter, *"It does not seem right that the public should be faced with ordeals of this nature, which in the case of women in delicate health, may lead to regrettable consequences. Only last summer a female inmate committed suicide by hanging herself in one of our woods.*

"Not long since, a male inmate belonging to a party being taken to a neighbouring church, threw himself under a motor omnibus and was killed in front of his companions; another female inmate got away from a party which had been taken to a cinema in Newport and drowned herself in the river; twice a tenant had to pull inmates out of his millpond; another tenant had to stop an inmate from throwing herself down his well, and a neighbour recently had a female inmate running through his house and frightening his children and servants."

In reply, Visiting Committee members said they were 'keenly alive to the difficulties attendant upon the Hospital's proximity to private residences'.

But despite this catalogue of suicides, they insisted the outings were 'conducive to the welfare and recovery of certain selected patients, and it would be in no way consonant with the trend of modern mental hospital administration to deviate from its present policy.'

The St Mary's site before the 'new' hospital was built. The old pauper burial ground is clearly visible as a darker area in the top right-hand corner of the picture

PAUPER GRAVES AT THE WORKHOUSE

Sevenacres, the new, purpose-built mental health unit on the St Mary's Hospital site, is a worthy successor to Whitecroft, for it too has acquired the reputation of being haunted. But Sevenacres was built in 1999 on fields off Dodnor Lane, so what could account for this? The supernatural trail leads back to the old Isle of Wight House of Industry, a complex of buildings known as the Workhouse or Poorhouse.

In the days before benefits and the Welfare State, this central workhouse, built on 80 acres of Crown land in 1774, was the last resort for the parish poor and unfortunate Islanders who fell upon hard times. Its function was 'to care for the aged and infirm, give employment to the able-bodied, correct the profligate and idle, and to educate the children in religion and industry'.

In its day, as the largest and most costly rural workhouse in the kingdom, it could accommodate up to 1,000 paupers. Some of the

The old Isle of Wight Workhouse is still part of the St Mary's Hospital complex

workhouse buildings are still in use today as part of lower St Mary's Hospital. (Read of hauntings here in *Ghosts of the Isle of Wight III*).

At the workhouse, the regime, discipline and punishments were harsh; food was basic. Men and women, even married couples, were segregated. Medical care of sorts was provided, and before Whitecroft was built, the workhouse also had 'Idiot Wards' and a 'home for the insane'. Records show an isolation unit known as the 'pest-house' for smallpox, typhoid, cholera and scarlet fever was built, with a separate ward for those suffering 'the Itch' - caused by lice, scabies or other infectious diseases.

Old House of Industry Registers make grim reading. Infant mortality rates were high and with so many people confined in close proximity, whole families were affected by epidemics of smallpox, typhoid and measles, which regularly swept through the poorhouse. In 1830, smallpox and measles carried off 94 children and adults. Between 1782 and 1858 - the period for which records are available, a total of 2,475 inmates were buried in the graveyard to the north of the workhouse off

Dodnor Lane. In all, a tremendous number of paupers were buried there in a haphazard jumble of unmarked graves. Few had headstones and virtually all records have been lost.

The first bodies were interred there in 1777 and when it filled up, the Bishop of Portsmouth consecrated more land. The last burials were in the 1940s, and in 1951 the burial ground, then disused, was levelled and used as a poultry run by a neighbouring farm.

When construction work on Sevenacres began, as a planning condition Kevin Trott of Wroxall carried out an archaeological watching brief, as the sensitive work of excavating and laying the new road started. Kevin explained that the purpose was to record the location of human remains disturbed during the work and have them reburied by an ordained person. At one metre deep, 19 graves were exposed, several still containing coffins. Some held children's remains and one tiny wooden coffin belonged to a baby. Kevin said that part of the sprawling burial ground had included a separate children's cemetery.

He added, "When I spoke to workmen during the road construction, they told me that when they laid land drains adjacent to Dodnor Lane, they had disturbed 'bones' which were re-buried during the backfilling of the drains. The graves and wooden coffins exposed by the works were protected when the new road's foundation was laid. The children's burial ground next to the car park has been protected and landscaped. All the remains were treated with proper respect."

GHOSTLY KNIGHT AT KITBRIDGE

On the edge of Parkhurst Forest stands Kitbridge Farm, an ancient holding once owned by Lord of the Island, Isabella de Fortibus, who kept her private militia there in the 13th century. The farm's history is long and intriguing. Nearby was the little leper hospital and chapel of St Augustine, which was served by the monks from St Mary's Priory. Its exact location is unknown today, but this 'maladeria' took patients with a variety of skin complaints, for the term 'leper' embraced many unsightly diseases. Today, one of those dedicated brothers who nursed the lepers is still around. For the ghost of a mendicant monk has been seen on a public footpath at Kitbridge by a man out walking his dog.

Its proximity to Albany Barracks and Parkhurst Military Hospital put Kitbridge at the heart of military activity. Officers were billeted at the farm and up to 10,000 troops could be camped nearby for exercises and

Kitbridge Farm near Parkhurst Forest where a ghostly knight has been seen

manoeuvres prior to leaving to fight overseas. In the build-up to the Peninsula War, the Isle of Wight was chosen as the biggest garrison in the whole country - probably because its isolation made desertion more difficult! On June 4th 1799, when the 10th Regiment was quartered at Newport, a review of 7,500 troops was held at Parkhurst Forest.

For long periods in its history, Newport was a lively garrison town with assemblies, reviews and even duels. Soldiers, military police and patrols were an everyday sight on the streets; many of the town's pubs reflected this military connection in their names. Entertaining and feeding thousands of soldiers contributed much to Island wealth, but Newport suffered the most unsavoury aspects of being an army town, such as drunkenness and prostitution.

Newport's Petticoat Lane, which ran between the town and Parkhurst also recalls the military presence, for it was named after the 'ladies of the night' who went there to meet soldiers and lift their petticoats for a few pennies.

Mark Earp, who has lived at Kitbridge Farm since 1961, has found ample evidence of military occupation around the farm. Armed with a metal detector, he is in the process of recording and researching these finds. Not only has he excavated a unique collection of insignia, badges, buttons, buckles, ammunition and artefacts - over 2,000 finds in a single field - he has also discovered a ghostly soldier. This shadowy officer on horseback is seen riding silently along the farm lane in the early hours of the morning.

In 1995, the farm whose modern exterior belies its origins, was renovated. "When we gutted the house we found the remains of a fortified medieval barn, which would have housed the family upstairs with the animals below. We also uncovered an old stone chimney breast and inglenook fireplace with a symbol of the Knights Templars cut into the stone. The secretive yet powerful medieval Templars were the most famous of the Christian military orders in the Middle Ages. Templar knights in their white tunic and red cross, some of the best equipped, trained, and disciplined fighting units of the Crusades, were once garrisoned at Carisbrooke."

So, is the ghostly knight which haunts Kitbridge one of these soldiers of Christ? Friends from Holland, who stayed at the farm, told Mark they had seen a ghostly presence wearing chain-mail one night, accompanied by a penetrating coldness. They left the very next morning and have not returned since.

When Laurel White, then aged 12, stayed in that room in 2005, she, too, met the ghost. Waking suddenly at 5am one summer morning, she saw the shadowy figure at the side of the bed. The room also appeared 'different'. A huge pot plant in front of the window was no longer there, furniture including the wardrobe and chest of drawers - everything but the bed Laurel was sleeping in, had vanished too. An incense burner now hung above the bed and smoke from this rose into the room.

"I saw a young man who didn't reflect any light. He was very thin, of medium height, with short hair. He wore a simple tunic top in brown and white, with tight trousers or leggings. I had been learning about the Middle Ages in school and he seemed to come from that time. He appeared to be watching himself in a looking-glass. He had a thin sword in his hand and was swishing and twisting it around in slow motion, as if posing with it.

"Then he paused, put the sword back in a scabbard at his waist, and started pacing up and down the room. He stopped and looked down at me for a few seconds, then went back to posturing with the sword in front of that invisible mirror. The pattern repeated itself. He put the sword away and paced the room. Then he stopped and looked at me again. He was about a metre from the foot of the bed. I don't know if he was aware of me. This time I shut my eyes, and when I heard the dogs downstairs barking, I screamed for Mark.

"The house is always cold but that morning the temperature had dropped sharply and it was freezing. As soon as Mark opened the door, the ghost disappeared bit by bit, then everything in the room was back to normal.

"Mark told me I had been dreaming, but later when we talked about what had happened, he told me other people had seen things in that room. I sleep in a different room now!"

Laurel's brother, Richard, was sleeping in a tent in the garden at Kitbridge one night when he heard the sound of an unseen presence walking round and round the house in heavy boots.

Mark himself has seen a bright aura of light appear on the wall in that room, which was formerly his bedroom, and has heard footsteps moving overhead and on the wooden stairs. "I think it is a good, protective ghost. The house has a friendly atmosphere - although two young men committed suicide in the attics there in the 19th century. There are no bad vibes here."

Today the farm is the headquarters of the Kitbridge Enterprises Trust, a nature reserve dedicated to great crested newts, where almost 100 ponds are being restored in former claypits there. Mark hopes the ghosts approve.

GHOST RIDERS IN THE MIST

One misty autumn morning in 2003, Penny Green set out to catch an early ferry. From her home at Norton Green, Freshwater, she drove along the Forest Road towards Newport. At 6am in the misty light of dawn, she noticed a string of six horses and riders emerge from Poleclose Lane ahead, and start to cross the empty road.

"I thought they were going for an early ride in the forest," Penny said. "Despite the mist I had the impression there were riders on the horses. Suddenly a motorcycle approached at speed from the opposite direction. The horses were still crossing. The motorcycle kept coming. It did not slow down at all. I was horrified because I thought it was going to plough into the horses, which were between the motorcycle and me. I gripped my steering wheel and waited for the inevitable accident.

"Suddenly the road was clear; the horses had disappeared; the motorcycle passed me; and as I went past the track into the forest that the horses had been heading for, it was empty. I don't know what I saw that day, but I cannot forget it."

Is this sighting an echo from this area's military past? A beautifully drawn and coloured military map now in the British Museum, details encampments at Newport in 1758 and 1759. Regiments are shown strung out in a long line from Poleclose farm, through Camp Hill to Horsebridge Hill. These pastures around Kitbridge were the usual area for quartering regiments. In those days, the forest would have been the natural place for these long-dead soldiers to take their horses for an early morning ride.

This engraving shows the Barracks at Parkhurst in 1836

The haunted Enchanted Manor at Niton Undercliff

Chapter Five

HAUNTINGS AT VENTNOR AND THE UNDERCLIFF

TRAGEDY IN THE FOG

Climb to the top of St Boniface Down and you are at the highest point on the Isle of Wight, some 787 feet above sea level, with spectacular views out to sea on a clear day. It was for this reason that a vital link in the top-secret wartime radar chain was built on the summit of St Boniface Down above Ventnor.

When tall pylons began appearing on the high downs, rumours started flying. Radio Direction Finding was in its infancy and the Island's part in this pioneering technology was one of its most vital contributions to the war effort. During construction of the four 350ft high steel radar towers in July 1939, one of the workers fell to his death. When hostilities began, the radar station - RAF Ventnor - became a target for heavy German bombardment and the town below suffered extensive damage and casualties as a result of these raids. The radar station and its pylons were badly damaged in two attacks by the Luftwaffe in 1940.

After the war, the RAF station at Ventnor became an important radar outpost, one of four covering the southern approaches to England. The site also contains an extensive bunker complex, now sealed, which was part of an early warning network. During the Cold War, it was converted for use as an administrative centre and shelter in case of nuclear attack.

It was here that one of the Island's worst plane crashes happened one gloomy May afternoon in 1962, when a Channel Airways Dakota aircraft struck the fog-shrouded southern face of St Boniface Down, just below the summit.

The plane bounced through the boundary fence of the RAF radar station, careered 250 yards uphill through the gorse and heather, striking the old buildings before coming to rest beside the road at the Island's highest point. Visibility in the low cloud was so appalling that a party of Civil Defence volunteers on an exercise, just 250 yards from the crash, were unaware of what had happened. It was left to a local man, who was picking bean sticks on the hillside, to demonstrate incredible bravery by entering the wreckage and rescuing survivors until the emergency services arrived.

Of the 17 people on board, seven survived the crash, but two died later in hospital. The crew perished with their passengers on the hillside. Among the dead were mothers, children, honeymoon couples and service personnel. Some survivors were in hospital for almost a year. When a memorial was dedicated to the accident over 120 people attended the ceremony, and it became clear that this tragedy had gone deep into the consciousness of people living on the Island at the time.

Some of the rescuers, both in the emergency services and civilians, were traumatised. Other witnesses and helpers still live with the memories. The fact that the wreckage (it was unrecognisable as an airliner) was left on the hillside for several days, caused nightmares for curious locals who came to see what had happened.

A memorial plinth and column now stand on St Boniface Down where those passing the crash site can read the plaque and reflect on what happened that day. With the passage of time, memories of the crash faded, but tales of ghosts at the crash site and the radar station nearby - especially when there's fog about - have not been laid to rest.

In the aftermath of the crash, the then National Air Traffic Control Services decided to extend radar cover across the Isle of Wight and the rest of the United Kingdom by constructing a series of long-range radar stations at strategic sites across the country. Ventnor was one of these.

In November 1964, John Langley, now retired and living with his wife Ann at Alverstone Garden Village, was transferred to the station from Manchester Airport as a Senior Air Traffic Engineer and duty officer. He spent several years working at the radar station. "It could be an odd place to work, particularly at night. Strange and inexplicable things could happen. People would hear 'noises' and many of those who worked at the station felt distinctly uncomfortable there at night.

"When the station was up and running, the radar could 'see' up to 180 nautical miles. Microwave links transmitted the radar pictures to London Airport from similar remote stations. Also at Ventnor we would listen out for the Alderney radio navigation beacon, coded ALD in Morse code. This had to be done every half hour, which was a real pain. If a red light came on to warn that the beacon had failed, a loud alarm bell would ring. We could silence the alarm with a key switch but the warning light remained on. We would then have to ring Southern Area Control Centre to tell them the beacon was off. The system always worked perfectly, until one night when I was on watch. There were four or five of us on duty at night, but most of the chaps took turns at going

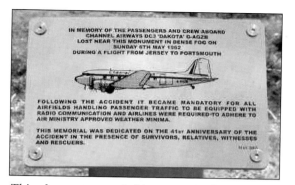

This plaque was erected in memory of those killed

to the rest-room for a nap. "I was sitting at the watchman's desk with the telephone and watch log. I looked across the room at dozens of racks of radar equipment and saw that the green light for Alderney was on. I was dozing when the telephone rang. It was Southern Area Control wanting to know if the Alderney beacon was still out of use. 'It's been an hour-and-a-half since you reported it out of service,' they insisted."

Puzzled, John looked in the logbook - there was no entry of any failure. All the other officers were asleep and no one had reported a beacon failure or red light. John tested the system immediately; the red light was on and the alarm key switch had been operated. The beacon was off the air! Who could have sent the warning for other aircraft?

"It was weird. It couldn't have happened, but it did. It was just one of the odd things that would occur there," said John. " For instance the station's Officer in Charge often brought Nicky, his golden labrador with him, but the animal would never go into the equipment room. There was an 'odd' feeling there and the dog would stand outside and bark. That room was never quiet. There were motors, fans and transformers whirring, but we would hear other noises too. Inexplicable noises. Footsteps when no one was there; a door banging - although it was locked.

"Headquarters later decided we needed a second radar scanner there. When the western end of the site and surrounding bushes were excavated for the foundations, we found half an engine and part of one of the Dakota's wings which had lain buried there since the crash.

"Today the site is run by National Air Traffic Services (NATS) but the old radars have long since gone. Airspace radar cover is provided by more modern and highly sophisticated systems throughout the UK. A radio communications service for Air Traffic Control and over-flying passenger aircraft still continues from St Boniface Down.

"But to this day, nobody can explain whether another incident similar to the Dakota tragedy was prevented by the mysterious message to London Air Traffic Control that night ...."

SOLDIER IN A DOORWAY

As a pre-history archaeologist, Laura Sullivan is used to dealing with the past. However it's not every day that she comes face to face with its ghosts. Although Laura, of High Street, Wroxall, has encountered ghosts before, she is still puzzled by two strange supernatural encounters.

The first was in the summer of 2004. Laura was walking up the hill from Ventnor seafront when she was astonished to see a man in khaki soldier's uniform sitting in a doorway at the corner of Albert Street. "It happened in a matter of seconds," she recalled. "I thought how odd it was because we don't have beggars on the Isle of Wight. He appeared to be in his late forties, on the elderly side for a soldier. Although the town was busy, no one else seemed to be aware of him.

"He appeared solid and real as he sat in the doorway - and did not look any too happy. He wore old-fashioned khaki uniform with boots, and a narrow folding cap. I took a few steps then looked back to check if he was all right. But the soldier was no longer there. He had vanished into thin air."

It was almost a year later, one July evening in 2005, when Laura had her next strange experience. This time it was at her Wroxall home. "It was growing dark when I looked out of the window to see the lower half of a man wearing a long, grey robe, gliding along as if he was being blown by the wind. He was going smoothly and quite fast, almost as though he was on wheels (which he wasn't). I think he was in view for about half a minute. I was so intrigued that I went to the next window to see where he had gone, but he had vanished. There was no traffic, no one else was around; the village was otherwise very quiet."

A GHOST FLUSHES THE TOILET

It's no joke when you find yourself sharing a bathroom with a ghost. But when Freddie Morris moved into a mews flat in Pound Lane, Ventnor, owned by the former South Wight Borough Council, he quickly discovered it was haunted. Between 1982 and 1984, he lived with his wife and newborn son at the old property which had sloping floors and a very ancient toilet.

Freddie recalls, "The first night I was there on my own, so I slept on a couch in the living room. At 2am I was woken by heavy footsteps coming up the passageway from the kitchen. I jumped up and opened the door, expecting to find an intruder. But no one was there. Then I heard the lavatory flush and when I ran in, the old-fashioned chain was still swinging in the empty room.

"Over the 18 months we lived there this happened regularly. It was very unnerving, for whenever we opened the door to see who was there, the room was empty, but the chain would be swinging gently....

"Sometimes when we were in the living room we would hear a man and woman arguing violently in the bedroom. We could never make out the words, but this ghostly couple were obviously having a row. They always seemed to be in the next room - I mean if we were in the bedroom, we could hear them in the living room. We would often hear footsteps in the hall, and the back door would open by itself, even when it was locked. I stopped this by fitting a heavy security chain.

"Finally we could stand it no longer. I asked the priest from St Wilfrid's Church to cleanse the flat. He brought some Holy water, which he sprinkled as he blessed the place. It didn't stop the ghostly activity completely, but it did cut it down considerably. After we left, another couple took our flat. We didn't mention the ghosts, but we later heard that as soon as they moved in, it all started up again. And a couple of months later when I went back to see if there was any post for us, they told me the flat was haunted! They were experiencing the same ghostly phenomena."

THE DOOMED EURYDICE

Ghost ships do still sail the treacherous waters off the Isle of Wight. One such phantom is HMS Eurydice, which capsized and sank in Sandown Bay in March 1878, during a sudden blizzard. Of the 366 men and boys aboard that afternoon, just two were saved. Eurydice, a 26-gun frigate, was returning to Portsmouth after a tour of Bermuda and the West Indies when disaster struck. Although later raised from Dunnose Point and beached on Bembridge Ledge, she was never re-commissioned. Her bell now hangs in St Paul's Church at Shanklin.

The sinking was witnessed by young Winston Churchill who was in Ventnor with his nurse. The four-year-old boy was watching from the cliffs when Eurydice capsized and a few days later he saw boats towing ashore bodies recovered from the wreck.

The ghost of James Turner, a 24-year-old marine who went down with the ship, later appeared at his sister's house, where it stood at her bedroom door with water dripping from wet clothing. Soon after the tragedy, fishermen and locals began to whisper of a three-masted ship, which would disappear when approached.

Since the sinking, several people claim to have seen this phantom ship. Many of these 'sightings' have been blamed on freak reflections of light on mist. But in 1930, Commander F. W. Lipscombe OBE ordered his submarine crew to take evasive action to avoid a three-masted, full-rigged sailing ship - which vanished as they watched. Commander Lipscombe was so intrigued by the incident that he later visited the Island, only to be told that he had seen the ghost of the doomed Eurydice.

Was it the Eurydice that Freddie Morris saw several times in the early 1980s? Freddie has seen ghosts since he was a boy, but even he was surprised by the appearance of the ghost-ship in Luccombe Bay.

At the time he was working at North Road Garage in Shanklin and living in Ventnor. "Many a night as I drove home I looked across the bay to see a three-masted ship which was lit up as if with fairy lights. I was always in the same spot when I saw it – just by the tearooms at Luccombe. I would sometimes go into the Volunteer Inn at Ventnor for a swift pint on the way home and one night, when I got talking to several old fishermen I asked, 'What's this old three-master I keep seeing out in the bay?'

"One of the men laughed and told me, 'Son, you'll often see that ship from Cowleaze Hill of a night, but when you get close you'll always lose sight of her. We have all seen her in the same place over the years. It's a proper mystery that one is'!"

GHOST IN A TOP HAT

On the very southernmost tip of the Island, not far from St Catherine's Lighthouse, is Knowles Farm, the home of Barry and Kathy Roberts since 1968. The property is ancient and appears in the Domesday Book.

Retired antique dealer Barry has done extensive work to the lonely, windswept stone property which is owned by the National Trust. When the couple moved there it had no electricity and during renovation work they found pictures of old sailing ships carved into the heavy wooden door. A regular beachcomber, Barry has found several bodies on the beach over the years. "A number of people have drowned or been washed ashore from wrecks here. I have found a fair few bodies myself!" He also discovered a smugglers' dead drop several years ago. This was revealed after a cliff fall one winter when Barry spotted an old wooden barrel sticking out of the cliff. Although the iron bands had rusted, the oak staves were still good. Sadly, any brandy, baccy, or lace once contained in the barrel was long gone...

In the cliffs nearby was a concealed cave, which was used to store tubs of contraband. Local folk insisted the cave was haunted, but tales of awful apparitions were probably spread by smugglers to keep curious folk away. The cave vanished in the great 1928 Blackgang landslip.

In 1860, poet Sidney Dobell who stayed at the nearby Royal Sandrock Hotel noted: *"The strange, wild, lawless life of the solemn, lawful-seeming people is an inexhaustible study. Here on St Catherine's Point, the most southern nose of Great Britain the whole population are smugglers. Everybody has an ostensible occupation, but nobody gets his money from it. Here are fishermen who never fish but always have pockets full of money; and farmers whose farming consists of ploughing the deep by night and whose daily time is spent in standing, like herons, on look-out posts. Nearly the whole village lives in masquerade, even to the names of the villagers. Hardly a man is known by his surname."*

The cosy, old stone farmhouse was haunted by the ghost of a man in a tall, grey top hat, who stood outside and tapped at the windows. "It went on for years," said Barry. "We became used to it." The family sometimes still hear sounds of a heavy object - a body perhaps - being dragged across the floor in the night, and light footsteps running across the landing, which sound like those of a child.

One of the strangest incidents at Knowles Farm involved a contractor who came to work at the nearby lighthouse. "We put him up for a few days in a room upstairs. But late one night we heard banging and shouting. The chap was in a complete panic and claimed 'someone' had got into bed with him. He ran out of the house, crossed the field to the lighthouse, then rushed up the tower. He was kicking out wildly at something invisible as he ran. Unfortunately he fell and broke his leg in the lighthouse tower. He didn't return to the house after that and we received an apology from Trinity House for his behaviour."

A local psychic arrived unexpectedly one day with a group of friends to expel the ghost, who she said had been drowned in a shipwreck off Atherfield Ledge in the 1840s. His earthbound spirit had roamed the cliffs ever since, she claimed.

Kathy however, was reluctant to allow them into the house. The ghost wasn't a nuisance and she was used to its presence. The psychics carried out their 'cleansing' from a nearby field. To Kathy's dismay, the tapping at the windows ceased after that and hasn't happened since.

This spirit may have been sent away, but in the cottage things still go inexplicably missing; bizarre and often bulky items, like a set of fire irons, which vanished from the huge inglenook fireplace in the sitting room. Currently a decorative silver hinge, which Barry was in the process of polishing, is still missing. Curiously, belts are another favourite target for whatever haunts the property, both at Barry and Kathy's home and next door, where retired nurse Sarah Frith lost a decorative silver nurse's buckle to the acquisitive spirit. Tools vanish regularly; some never return. One hefty garden rake never came back. Usually however, the objects do turn up again, sometimes weeks or months later, and often in the same place they vanished from.

Neither Barry and Kathy nor Sarah, who lived next door for nine years, mind the hauntings - though Sarah was once locked out by her ghost. After going into the garden, she found herself locked out. The heavy key in the mortice lock had been turned and Barry had to use a hammer on the door to open it for her.

Sometimes Sarah heard a woman's light tread on the staircase at night, and in August 2004 she also heard a man's heavy footsteps walking around, but no one was ever there.

Over a century ago, this area was used by radio pioneer, Guglielmo Marconi, for his experiments and on January 23rd 1901, radio waves transmitted from the Knowles Farm station travelled nearly 200 miles to be picked up by the Lizard Radio Station in Cornwall. Marconi had achieved the world's first long distance radio transmission. His huge aerial was erected in the front garden in 1900 and even today, Barry digs up fragments of old battery core. At Knowles Farm a stone is cut with the following inscription, *"This is to commemorate that Marconi set up a wireless experimental station here in AD 1900"*.

THE ENCHANTED MANOR

For over a century Wind Cliff at Niton was home to members of the wealthy Kirkpatrick family. In the 1960s, it became an hotel, Windcliffe Manor, and in 2007 began a new incarnation as The Enchanted Manor. While the owners, décor and name have changed, its ghosts have not.

This old aerial view of Niton Undercliff and Blackgang shows St Catherine's lighthouse with Knowles Farm just behind

Wind Cliff was built in 1837 by the prominent banking family of James, Joseph and Edward Kirkpatrick who also owned the Manor of Niton and many neighbouring estates and farms, as well as St Cross House in Newport. Wind Cliff was given to Miss Kirkpatrick as a wedding present and as the newly-married Mrs Prendergast, she used the Niton house as her summer residence. She was a keen gardener and laid the foundations of the beautiful gardens there. When she was widowed, Mrs Prendergast lived out her days as a recluse at Wind Cliff.

At least two ghosts haunt the old house. One is a gentleman in Edwardian dress, the other a gentle ghost, believed to be the spirit of Mrs Prendergast herself. Former owners Jean and David Heron, who bought Windcliffe Hotel in 1988 made the ghosts' acquaintance soon after moving in. The sound of voices was heard in one of the empty bedrooms and footsteps climbed the stairs when no one was around. A figure in white was seen walking across the hall, always in August, and usually at the same time each year. This ghost triggered the alarm system and would frequently switch the lights off.

When they were sitting quietly downstairs, the Herons would sometimes hear those footsteps pattering softly around in empty rooms overhead. Guests in one of the bedrooms heard the unseen presence sighing deeply as it moved along the landing at the dead of night. In that haunted bedroom - once the billiard room - a phantom figure in Edwardian costume was seen at the foot of the bed.

Mrs Prendergast's spirit showed a particular interest in sewing machines. Even with the electricity switched off at the mains, the Heron's sewing machine would start on its own, the needle running faster and faster.

Subsequent owners discovered a ghostly presence playing with the billiard balls in the games room, where the unmistakable click of balls was heard late at night. Perhaps the ghost was enjoying a frame on the hotel's magnificent billiard table.

When Maggie Hilton first saw Windcliffe Manor Hotel, she was so enchanted by its welcoming atmosphere that she and Ric, her Australian husband, bought it at auction in October 2006. Working their magic they gave the hotel a fairytale makeover, transforming it into The Enchanted Manor, with unique fantasy artwork, seven sumptuous four-poster suites and a woodland garden.

"The house needed to be loved and brought back to life. There is such a lovely feeling here, that the ghosts are obviously friendly," said Maggie. From the outset they took a great interest in the project. James, who became Ric and Maggie's 'Mr Fixit', has seen and heard them many times. As a former serviceman, James has a practical and sceptical nature, but even he puts the strange happenings at the hotel down to the supernatural.

James said, "I have been working here alone at night and heard the sound of footsteps on a wooden floor upstairs. They were light footsteps, a woman's, I believe. The second I got to the room they stopped. I have also heard the footsteps in the hallway, and smelled a woman's perfume.

"It was there suddenly, a strong, flowery musky scent, the sort an elderly lady would wear. It was so powerful that you could move in and out of the smell. Suddenly it disappeared as quickly as it arrived. I noticed it quite a few times, and Mark, the decorator, smelled it as well on the landing and in the corner bedroom. Ric just laughed at us and thought it was a great joke – until he smelled it for himself."

Often those phantom footsteps would be heard at 8pm but one evening when James sat on the stairs waiting for them, nothing happened. Later however, he found the main door had been wedged open. "The temperature dropped suddenly and I felt icy cold. I trained in Norway so I am used to extreme cold, but this was something else.

Suddenly, as I watched, the door slammed shut and took the wedge with it .... then slowly opened on its own again.

"In March 2007 I was working in the kitchen one morning when I heard doors open and close. Again, there was no one there. Another day I was in the front vestibule drilling holes in the wall for a display stand when 'something' grabbed me by the shoulder.

Mrs Prendergast's spirit still haunts her old home

I jumped back dropping the drill, and spun round. No one was there.

"It became increasingly obvious that 'something' didn't want me drilling into the wall, because it took me most of the day to bore a four-inch hole into a sandstone wall and put a screw in there. Finally, the screw snapped and I gave up.

"Lights are switched off and on when I am here on my own. I am used to it now. One day I called out, 'Oh there you are again Henrietta'. I don't know where the name came from, it just popped into my mind. I even got a Christmas card for her this year. I get a very strong sense of her presence, she is friendly, and clearly interested in what we are doing to 'her' home."

Cowes medium Leslie George confirmed this when he visited the hotel a few days after it re-opened in May 2007. Les 'saw' several spirits at The Enchanted Manor, including a gardener from the early 1900s who continues to move to and fro between the house and some sheds in the gardens (which no longer exist).

On entering the house, Les said, "We are being watched by two brothers, aged about 14 and 16. They are both very well-to-do and are smartly dressed in Edwardian clothing. Their names start with the initial D, and they are good-natured, fun-loving spirits. They are pranksters and I feel that they are responsible for many of the things that happen and for things being moved downstairs. I see them peering around doorways, taking an interest in guests and what goes on. They generally remain downstairs.

"The other spirit is a lady from the 1840s in a beautiful rich brocade costume in maroon or mauve, with full petticoats and skirt. She clearly has plenty of money, and this was - and still is - her house. She usually stays on the first and second floors where she checks everything is in its place. She often watches from the windows and although she is aware of the two boys, I don't think they are aware of her.

"She keeps a close eye on any changes and alterations to the house and is happy with what has been done here. There is an overwhelmingly good feeling; the hotel and its gardens are a peaceful and spiritual place. The ghosts are content here and don't want to leave."

Visit The Enchanted Manor at: *www.enchantedmanor.co.uk*

Chapter Six

GHOSTS OF OLD GODSHILL

Five miles south of Newport lies the picturesque village of Godshill, famous for its thatched cottages, cream teas and ancient hilltop church. By day its shops and tea gardens bustle with tourists. By night when the visitors have gone, it's time for the ghosts to come out...

SPIRITS AT THE CASK AND TAVERNERS

The Cask and Taverners, one of two pubs left in Godshill, was once the village bakery. Here, a ghostly woman's figure moves from the old bakery in the rear, through the bar, to the front of the building, which at one time served as a grocery and Post Office. The pub opened as the Taverners Restaurant in the late 1970s and was later extended to incorporate the courtyard into the present bar area.

A number of people, both customers and staff, report a 'strange feeling' in the area of the washrooms and some won't use those toilets at all. Just before Christmas 2005, John Beaumont who became licensee in 2004, was alone and locking up. "I went to the Gents to check everything was secure. As I walked out I had a sensation of tingling like pins and needles all over my body. I felt electrified. It only lasted for about a minute as I stood on the threshold of the old bakery."

Chris Austin of West Street, Godshill, has seen the ghostly lady twice. On the first occasion the figure was near the restaurant door. "A generously proportioned middle-aged woman, about 5ft 10ins tall, she wore a long, old-fashioned dress and white apron. I couldn't see her feet. Her grey hair was tied back off her face in a bun.

"She stood with arms folded and as I looked at her out of the corner of my eye, she looked back at me. We gazed at one another for about twenty seconds. During that time she didn't move. She reappeared about half an hour later, sitting in a (modern) chair. This time she was visible for about ten seconds. She looked at me in a challenging way, as if to say, 'this is my place and I am still here keeping an eye on things'. She was seen again the next night by two locals."

Another regular, who has also worked at the pub, described the ghost as looking 'all grey'. The figure wore a long dress or skirt with a long white pinny, and appeared 'slightly hunched'.

Although he has not seen them, Chris has sensed the spirits of two ghostly children who play in the old courtyard (now part of the main bar area). He is also aware of a man's angry spirit in the rear of the building. "This man doesn't approve of anything modern. He doesn't like electricity and tampers with equipment there, including the fruit machines and lights."

Lyn and Adrian Fagg received a spooky welcome when they took over the pub in January 2007. "When I arrived, I could feel the place was haunted by two very different spirits," said Lyn. "There is a sense of cold, and we hear thuds and groans at the lower end of the pub where the old bakery was. This feels like a man's energy. The other presence at the front of the building is much lighter, warmer and definitely female. When my barmaid Karen and I were alone here after closing time, the lights began to flicker, and the atmosphere went icy cold. There was a feeling of such sadness that when Karen and I looked at one another, we both had tears in our eyes."

Lyn has also seen the spirit of a small girl in a cream dress skipping around the courtyard outside. "A lady who works here arrived with her granddaughter - or so I thought, for I saw a child with her. When I went to greet them the little ghost-girl vanished."

OLD MR BELLAMY

Whoever haunts Godshill's Natural History Museum and Shell collection is obsessed with locks and keys. At this visitor attraction, established in 1965, what appears to be an imposing Victorian red-brick house is only a façade concealing an ancient stone cottage behind it. The old cottage was built in 1630 and had become derelict by the 1960s. It underwent extensive renovations before opening as the Coral View Tropical Shell Collection. It was established by shell collector and geologist, Mr C. L. Bellamy, a Fellow of the Conchological Society of Great Britain. Together with some 12,000 shells, the museum houses minerals, fossils, semi-precious stones and, surprisingly, stained glass windows from the former (haunted) Royal National Hospital at Ventnor, which are incorporated into the entrance hall.

When the present owners bought the museum and collections in 1995, they were soon convinced the building was haunted. They are not sure who their ghost is, but have their suspicions!

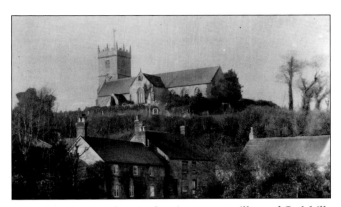

There are ghosts galore in the picturesque village of Godshill

"At first we had all sorts of strange things going on, but as the years go by, our ghost has settled down. When we first moved here we did some work which obviously disturbed him."

Certain areas of the building can suddenly feel cold, very cold, and often, when locking up at the end of the day, the owners are convinced that someone - or something - is in the museum with them.

Often things will go missing, only to turn up again somewhere obvious. "Our ghost likes keys and locks in particular. When we first moved here, we would often lose the keys to the building. They would always turn up again in exactly the middle of the hallway. We even measured it once, and yes, they were in precisely the centre of the floor.

"The front door has two padlocks, top and bottom, and sometimes at night, and for no reason, they both start to swing in perfect unison, then the movement will stop suddenly. Sensitive and psychic visitors sometimes comment, 'This place is haunted; there's something here.' Some young visitors may agree, for occasionally a child will start to cry, or run out of the museum in tears for no reason that anyone can fathom, refusing to be comforted. We sometimes wonder whether old Mr Bellamy is still around, keeping an eye on his precious collection of shells. Could he be ticking off those children who try to touch them?"

GHOSTLY PRESENCE AT THE COTTAGE

Across the road from the shell museum is a charming 17th century farm cottage, which was rebuilt after a fire in the early 1970s. In Edwardian times, it was a tea garden run by two sisters, the Misses Firth. Today, as a herb garden and gift shop, The Cottage is a popular visitor attraction, and it, too, is haunted. Alvin Brooks and his staff have heard ghostly footsteps overhead, as if someone was walking on bare floorboards. "We can go for weeks without anything happening, then we clearly hear a woman's footsteps crossing the empty room upstairs. It happens several times a year.

"We have had visitors comment on a 'presence' here. One psychic woman actually told us, 'Don't be frightened but there is an elderly lady in a long dress who sits in a chair in the corner in what was once her home. She is happy and is a benign presence. She sits on the left hand side of the room in the back corner and just keeps an eye on things' …"

THE HAUNTED BAT'S WING

When you visit the Bat's Wing, if you want to share your meal with a ghost, don't forget to ask for table number three - it's the haunted one!

It's probably the most unusual property in the village. Set in Church Hollow at the foot of Church Hill, this thatched cottage built in 1536, was once two separate dwellings. Now a popular tearoom, run since 1998 by Pauline Williams and her daughter Julia Warne, the Bat's Wing has also been an antiques shop, grocery and colonial store, museum and gift shop, as well as serving as a doctor's house and surgery in the 1800s.

There's a deep cellar under the property, once used to house the parish canon which every parish was obliged to have during the reign of Henry VIII, to defend against invasion. It is also said that a tunnel leading from the Bat's Wing cellar to the church at the top of the hill was used by priests in hiding. Stonework believed to be from the tunnel entrance still exists there.

The Bat's Wing has long had the reputation of being haunted. Previous owners Jean and David Heron, heard ghostly footsteps and voices, and soon after Pauline and Julie took over, they noticed the occasional extra customer at table number three.

"You think someone has come in, you see them from the corner of your eye, but when you look more closely, there's no one there," said Pauline. "One afternoon we had four people sitting at that table; two men and their wives. One of the men, sitting with his back to us, asked my husband John, 'Have you got a ghost in here?'

"John laughingly told him, 'Oh yes, she sits where your wife is!' The customer said, 'Actually I believe you, because something has just touched me on the shoulder'."

In July 2007, another visitor, taxi driver and developing medium David Hughes of Staffordshire, told Pauline that he sensed the spirits of two clergymen, called George and Francis, perhaps friars or monks, for he saw them carrying rosary beads. David also saw the spirit of an elderly lady named Rose, who haunts the Bat's Wing. Rose who is in her eighties, is content to remain there and is happy with what has been done to 'her' old home, he told Pauline. David added, "There is a warm, welcoming feeling at the Bat's Wing. I think Rose

A ghost called Rose haunts the Bat's Wing at Godshill

was once involved with a bakery here, for I get the smell of baking bread. She wears a long black dress, probably from early Victorian times, and a white apron looped at her shoulders, reaching down to the floor. Her hair is grey and pulled back in a bun. I see her sitting in a rocking chair with a ginger cat asleep on her knee.

"Rose lost her husband at sea and she often stands upstairs looking out of the front window. She puts a candle in a glass at the window as if trying to show him the way home. She stays in the tearooms and sits at table three, because that's where her rocking chair once was."

Other visitors have remarked that something touches their head, and Pauline has experienced this herself. She has also felt that tap on the shoulder.

"In the shop one day I was looking out of the window when I felt someone touch my shoulder. There's nothing unpleasant about it. This is such a warm and friendly place, I have a sense that whatever haunts it is female. I do talk to her sometimes, and I always say goodnight to her. It's good manners."

John had a close encounter with the Bat's Wing ghost in bed one night. In their bedroom, which is at the front of the building overlooking the street, he was just dropping off to sleep when he suddenly sat up with a cry and shot out of bed. The door from the staircase opened and an invisible presence touched him on the back, John told his astonished wife when she asked what the matter was.

"We sometimes hear someone moving about downstairs in the early hours, and have found chairs moved around. Once we discovered the sauce bottles had moved across the room. We hear a door open and close in the night - very faintly, and sometimes we hear the kettle in the kitchen being switched on and off. Perhaps our ghost makes herself a cup of tea!

"A number of people who come here say they sense a presence, and they all agree it's a friendly one. As to the Bat's Wing name, no one knows how it originated.

"Some say it is because of the shape of the thatched roof at the front facing the street. Perhaps it is because of the number and variety of bats flitting about Church Lane at night."

However the name originated, the Bat's Wing is a charming place serving delicious cream teas, and when you go there, be sure to ask for table number three!

THE CHURCH HILL GHOST

Old villagers tell of a young woman who was murdered long ago on Church Hill. It's said that on a dark moonless night, if you listen carefully, you'll hear the swishing sound of her long skirts, as she tries to flee her killer.

This ghost may not be alone in her wanderings, for the spirit of a monk walks here too. Owners of the Bat's Wing sometimes hear the sound of heavy footsteps on the path beside their windows between 4am and 5am.

The lane is empty however. Perhaps the ghostly cleric is on his way to an early morning service at the church.

It's likely that plague victims from the Black Death, which swept the Island in the 14th century, may well have been buried in pits nearby. The plague which devastated Godshill spared just 13 villagers.

Lightning Strikes

Godshill seems to attract lightning strikes. The church has frequently been struck, with devastating consequences. It was hit in the great storm of 1778, again in 1897, and in January 1904 lightning did such damage that the tower had to be dismantled and rebuilt, stone by stone. A 70ft high granite obelisk standing 685ft above sea level on top of the down above Godshill was badly damaged by a lightning strike in 1831. Despite this, Godshill was the last Island village to get electricity! Not until 1956 was it finally connected, relying until then on gas for cooking and lighting.

All Saints Church

A dozen churches in England attract 100,000 plus visitors a year. All Saints at Godshill is one of this select few. The current church dating from the fourteenth century is the fourth on the site. Once it was the richest church on the Island, its walls painted with biblical scenes in vibrant colours; traces have been found under plaster on all the walls.

Here the soft chant of ghostly voices has been heard, and the sound of phantom footsteps occasionally disturbs the silence. In 2005, a novice bellringer who was recording her practice captured the sound of a deep ghostly voice on tape, which is heard complaining 'I'm so tired'.

Church Hill was probably once a place of pagan worship. Legend tells that the first church was founded in the eighth century when a holy man arrived to convert people to Christianity. His mission was a spectacular success and villagers agreed to build a church. A site was chosen to the south of the village, the foundations marked out and huge stones piled one upon another. At nightfall the villagers stopped to rest. They awoke to an astonishing sight. Mysteriously the stones had been moved to the top of the hill. Undeterred, the builders tried again to put up their church. Again, as they slept, the stones were spirited away to the hilltop. After three nights, the builders took the hint and decided it was God's will for the church to be built atop the hill. The ground was duly consecrated and work on the hilltop church began. And thus God's Hill became Godshill.

It may just be coincidence that the land originally earmarked for the church at the foot of the hill was owned by a farmer with few, if any, religious convictions. He strongly objected to the building of a place of Christian worship, arguing that he was unworthy of such an honour because of his many sins. He became the prime suspect and local people decided to call the land 'rejected' by the stones the Devil's Acre, a name by which it is still known today.

The Old Bell Inn

The cottages near the church entrance were probably built in the 15th century, possibly to house masons rebuilding the church. Nearby, Old Bell Cottage features in many postcards and calendars of Godshill. However few people today realise this picturesque thatched cottage was once a notorious bawdy alehouse and the original village inn. Saturday nights were the worst and elderly villagers remember that after a hard night's supping at the Bell Inn, those drinkers who passed out, or were unable to find their way home, were laid out to sleep it off on the grassy bank nearby, much to the horror of devout churchgoers on Sunday mornings.

The inn closed in the 1920s, to the relief of neighbours who kept pails of water by the bedroom window to throw over rowdy drinkers in the early hours. The local constabulary raided the premises at intervals, always without success. Whether the landlord was 'tipped off' no one will say, but the police never managed to catch anybody drinking there after hours!

The old Bell Inn on Church Hill which was closed down in the 1920s

OLD TOM'S GHOST

One of a dwindling band of 'old' villagers, retired builder and carpenter Gordon Cooke was born in Pound Cottage on Church Hill. One of the oldest cottages in Godshill dating back to the early 1600s, this picturesque dwelling was haunted by a gentle ghost known affectionately by the family as 'Alice'.

"Often the latch on the door between the kitchen and lounge would lift on its own, and mother would call out 'Stop that, Alice!' We never saw her and don't know who she was. Although she usually confined herself to those two rooms, her footsteps were heard on the stairs at night when the cottage was quiet."

Growing up in Pound Cottage, Gordon recalls that until 1935 water for drinking, cooking, and heating the old copper boiler, was drawn from a well at least 85 feet deep, outside the back door. "When I was a lad there were just 500 people in Godshill Parish and you knew who all your neighbours were. Nearby on Church Hill, our neighbour old Tom Hollis lived in a two room cottage. Every morning when my father started up his old model 'T' Ford and set off to work on the farm, old Tom would be at the window with a cheery wave.

"One day, my father set off as usual, exchanging waves with old Tom. Returning home for dinner, my mother met him with the sad news that Tom had passed away the previous night. Father insisted this couldn't be true, for the old man had been at his usual place to wave him off that morning! 'Well, it must have been his ghost then, because the poor old chap was stone dead at the time,' mother replied."

LADY IN BLACK

Now a popular family pub, the Griffin was built by Lord Yarborough, owner of Appuldurcombe House, in the early nineteenth century. This magnificent weathered grey stone building with its tall angular chimneys and carved stone griffin, has been extended over the years without losing its charm. When Licensee Andy Steele moved there in 1997 he carried out major alterations to the old coaching inn, which caused consternation to the ghosts.

In the kitchen, chef Mark, who was on his own there couldn't find the day's menu list. "I searched everywhere," he said. "Then I turned round to find it in a box of cucumbers. When I tried to pick it up, the list wouldn't budge, for it had been stabbed through with a pen which was stuck into a cucumber. It was bizarre. Later, the list vanished completely. I never found it again."

Locals knew the pub was haunted, but not who the ghost was. Alan Jones from Ward Close, Newport, was working as a barman in September 2005, when he had a close encounter with a lady in black. Alan recalled, "When I started work there I asked other staff if the place was haunted. Quite a few employees told me they had seen the ghost themselves and everyone described the same thing – a woman in black who walked through the building and disappeared.

"After a few months I realised I didn't like a particular area of the old pub. The mirror above the old stone fireplace made me very uneasy for no good reason. Then one evening I found out why.

"It was late one wet night in September and I was finishing up behind the bar. All the customers had gone; I was alone and waiting for Andy, the owner, to get back before I could go home. Standing behind the bar, I looked up to see the dark, shadowy figure of a woman on the other side of the bar. She wore a black Victorian dress and she had a very prominent, hooked nose. I froze.

"I didn't know what to do. I was pretty sure that what I was looking at was a ghost and it seemed to be the same one other staff had described. As I watched, the figure disappeared. Just to be on the safe side, I walked around the other side of the bar, as far away from where I had last seen her as possible, and began to get on with something to keep busy. A few moments later I glanced up again, and this time, the ghost was walking across the bar towards the fireplace with the mirror above. As she reached it, she turned slowly, looked right at me, and vanished again.

"Some ten minutes passed, and although I was still alone in the place, I began to relax a little. Suddenly there was a movement, and out of the corner of my eye I saw something grey shuffling up to the bar. Then it spoke. I turned around quickly, only to discover one of the regulars had come in. I laughed out loud in relief.

"But seeing that he was the only customer in the bar, he didn't want to stay, and went home, leaving me alone once more with the ghost. It was another 40 minutes before Andy arrived and I could go home myself."

Alan added, "There is a particular spot behind the bar which will suddenly grow freezing cold, although there's no draught there." While

A ghostly lady in black haunts the popular Griffin Family Inn at Godshill

Alan was standing behind the bar one afternoon with a friend, he suddenly noticed one of the children's high chairs needed a clean. "I picked up a cloth and walked towards it. As I did so, the little red footrest flew off and landed right at my feet - as if something was trying to be helpful. There was no one nearby - no one we could see anyway."

Although Andy, the licensee, has never seen the ghost himself, other members of his staff and occasional customers certainly have. The Lady in Black, as she's known, walked past barmaid Gemma one morning when she was behind the bar programming the tills. Later that afternoon, a customer sitting with his family insisted he could see a lady in black. "I'm telling you I can see her," Andy heard him telling his disbelieving wife and daughter, who clearly saw no one there. The visitors were sitting at a table by the fireplace and that mirror.

Another staff member, also called Gemma, watched in amazement one day as an empty glass shot off the bar and landed several feet away by the pool table, where it shattered. So the next time you pop into the Griffin, keep an eye open for the 'Lady in Black'.

Haunted Staplehurst Grange at Newport, pictured here during a livestock sale in the 1920s, is better known today as the Isle of Wight Lavender Farm

Chapter Seven

SPIRITS OF NEWPORT

LAVENDER AND GHOSTLY MONKS

It's now known as Staplers but originally this area of high ground to the north east of Newport was called Staplehurst. The medieval Grange of Staplehurst has been in the Abbott family since 1927. The farm occupies 183 acres of unspoilt countryside and ancient woodland where rare orchids, dragonflies and butterflies flourish.

Today it is the successful Isle of Wight Lavender Farm, but in the 12th century the Grange, one of the wealthiest monastic farms on the Island, was owned by the Cistercian Abbey of Quarr.

This once-struggling beef farm has been transformed by the aptly-named Abbott family into a Royal Horticultural Society award-winning enterprise. The buildings have been converted by brothers Paul and Reuben Abbott, into a lavender distillery, cosmetics shop and popular tea-rooms, where visitors can indulge in the excellent lavender scones and shortbread.

The ghosts there obviously approve of the changes, for a phantom monk paused to watch Reuben and Paul as they repaired the roof of an old barn. "A couple of visitors observed a ghostly monk walk into the courtyard and pause to watch us working on the old roof, before vanishing," said Paul.

And just a day after starting work in the tea-rooms in March 2007, Harriet Young was startled to see a brown-clad and hooded figure vanishing round the corner by that barn.

Could this be the same hooded figure that their grandmother, Joyce Cheek, drove *through* when coming home one night in the late 1930s? Paul explained, "Granny could 'see things' and she was coming up the lane when this hooded monk walked right *through* the car. On another occasion when she got up to see why her children were crying one night, she saw a white, sheet-like figure pass through the bed."

Paul and Reuben often 'lose' tools - only for them to reappear a while later. They call this mischievous, light-fingered spirit 'Foogie'. Occasionally they also smell the familiar pipe smoke of their grandfather Edwin Cheek, which evokes a great feeling of nostalgia. Reuben said,

"You can walk into one of the greenhouses and it smells as if he is standing next to you, puffing away. That's nice! I often sense him around and talk to him about what I have been doing and what's going on. He was full of fun. It's good to know he's keeping an eye on things here."

A little black and white ghost-dog with a long tail is also seen about the place, and as a young child, Charlotte Abbott would wake in the night to hear him panting next to her on the bed. "Years ago we did have a little black and white Jack Russell – and she was the only one allowed on our bed!" said Paul. "Actually Charlotte is very sensitive, when she was aged two, we would hear her chattering away to someone when she was alone. She insisted she was talking to 'my grandfather' and when she described him, her description matched that of our granddad Edwin."

Paul's wife, Jackie, added, "Whatever is here is more active if visitors are in the house. When my mum and dad, Bob and Chris, came to stay in 2005 to look after the place while we were away, odd things happened. Mum was on the sofa labelling candles for the shop when one of them flew across the room. Other things were continually being moved and doors all over the house were opened. Mum and dad thought they were going mad. We keep packets of photos on the top shelf of a cupboard in the sitting room. One morning, dad got up to find the door to the room wide open and the photos all over the living room floor. When mum saw what had happened she spoke out loud to the ghost, 'We are just looking after the house while Paul and Jackie are on holiday. Please leave us alone.'

"Another time, Reuben and Jill looked after the house when we were away. They also found objects being moved. One night Reuben's wellington boots disappeared from the kitchen and were left in the centre of the living room floor."

Jackie often finds lights switched on in their bedroom when no one has been there. This is the same room in which Paul's grandmother saw the white figure, and when their son Thomas slept there, he woke to see the ghost of a young girl standing silently, watching him. He thought at first that it was his sister, Charlotte. She, however, was fast asleep.

Thomas recalled, "Something woke me, and this girl was there, standing just outside the door on the landing. She looked a bit like my sister, but she was wearing black clothes and her eyes appeared red. She looked at me so I said 'Charlotte is that you?' Then I realised I could see right *through* her. I turned the light on and she vanished, but when I

Staplehurst Grange was once owned by Quarr Abbey

switched it off, she was back again." Paul added, "This is the room great-grandmother died in, but there is no feeling of menace at all. In fact the place has a very peaceful and welcoming feeling. This was a wonderful place to grow up and we had an amazing childhood. We are close to Newport but very hidden away here - it's like stepping back in time. Staplehurst Grange is a very special place and we have tried to keep it so. We like to think that whatever ghosts are here approve of what we are doing with 'their' farm. A few years ago we had it blessed by Abbot Cuthbert of Quarr Abbey. Since then the place has felt happier."

It's especially appropriate that Staplehurst Grange, the former monastery holding, has become a lavender farm. After the Romans brought lavender to England it was grown extensively by monks as part of their physic gardens where they grew a range of herbal remedies. Lavender soon entered English folklore; a lavender cross was often hung on the door to ward off evil spirits and during the Plague people tied lavender bunches to their wrists.

MEALS ON WHEELS GHOST

In Staplers Road is the old Island headquarters of the Women's Royal Voluntary Service. Owned by the WRVS for many years, this house was previously used by the town's 'Moral Welfare Association'. Two ghosts were seen there over many years. One was known as 'Charlie', the other, a young girl who stayed in the attics, had no name, but staff would hear ghostly footsteps and movement in empty rooms upstairs.

When the late Mrs Morris worked as a volunteer there, Charlie was seen moving about the old house. One day in 1985, she asked her son Freddie, who has seen spirits since he was a small child, to go up into the attic to fetch some coathangers.

"I think it was a pretext to see what I could 'pick up'," said Freddie. "We heard a loud bump overhead so I quickly went upstairs. I was immediately aware of the spirit of a man, dressed in a dark suit with a white wing collar, standing on the landing. I feel that he was an overseer of some sort. Charlie seemed to be a figure of authority, and I sensed he was annoyed at having strangers in his domain.

"I said politely, 'Excuse me, Charlie' and went past him upstairs into the attics where there was a rocking chair facing the dormer window. The atmosphere felt 'charged' and I could see the spirit of a teenage girl sitting in the chair. She seemed very sad and lonely as she gazed out of the window across the rooftops of Newport."

Pat Chaplin-Orman of Winford, who ran the Meals on Wheels Service from her second floor office in the old building, confirms that the haunting there was well-known by staff and volunteers. "One ghost was said to be a young woman who once lived in a room in the attics and worked at the old Broadlands lace factory opposite. She was in love with a handsome young man, but this affair ended in tragedy when he died. Her unhappy spirit was said to sit in that top room watching in vain for his return.

"There was definitely a presence there. I felt it on a number of occasions, although I never saw anything. When working alone there, I would hear the faint sound of a door closing overhead, and a single footstep. It was a friendly ghost, though a touch light-fingered, for we often used to lose things, particularly keys, papers and documents. They usually came back eventually though," added Pat.

The ghosts must have moved on, for today the old house is occupied by a firm of insurance brokers, whose staff report all is quiet there now.

HOODED GUILDHALL GHOST

Mervyn Jelley doesn't believe in ghosts, so when he saw one walk through the doors to Newport's ancient Guildhall, he was, in his words, rather 'taken aback'.

It was Autumn 2004 and the time was 3.55am. Mervyn who was working on night security at Calvert's Hotel, had just stepped outside when he noticed a tall, hooded person moving outside the Guildhall opposite. In the streetlight, he saw the figure was wearing a dark grey hooded cape reaching down to the ground.

"About ten feet away across the road I could see the figure quite clearly. As I stopped, so did he, although he made no sound. He was about 6ft 2ins tall, but I couldn't see his face. There was just an empty blackness where the face should have been.

"I thought it was a drunk or someone larking around at that time in the morning. The odd figure moved again, and then it vanished under the Guildhall arches, emerging into Quay Street.

Old Newport Guildhall where a tall, hooded figure is seen

Here it briefly paused before walking *through* the side doors and disappearing. I was surprised because I didn't think those doors were used any more," said Mervyn.

"I got my torch and went across to see if they were unlocked. However, I saw that those cobweb-encrusted doors had not been opened in a very long time. I have never believed in ghosts but I know what I saw that night, and I can't explain it any other way."

Is this mysterious figure connected with the sound of footsteps heard moving along the stone corridors at Newport Guildhall, once the Island's 'Old Bailey' and market place? For centuries, the Guildhall, now a museum and Tourist Information Centre, stood at the centre of the ancient Borough of Newport. It was a multi-purpose building housing law courts, town hall and market place. Ancient charters show the site has been used for local government since the Middle Ages. The present building was designed by John Nash in 1816 and cost £10,000. It replaced earlier buildings dating from 1406 and 1639. Many people have stood trial here and those walls have witnessed dark and terrible secrets. The sound of deliberate heavy footsteps moving between the old courtrooms is still heard at night. Now retired, John Short, who spent many years as hallkeeper, knew those footsteps well. "You would only hear them when the courts had all adjourned, and the building was empty at night."

THE WALKING DEAD AT COUNTY HALL

It was after 5pm one Friday afternoon in July 2007 when Linda met one of the ghosts of Newport's County Hall. The middle-aged woman dressed all in black, looked as though she was going to a funeral.

Linda (not her real name), who had just finished her shift in the council's call centre, emerged from the second floor ladies' cloakroom off the building's 'middle' staircase. She was surprised to see the woman coming downstairs, for staff had left and the building was almost deserted.

Dressed in a very old-fashioned black costume with black shoes, looking as though she was in mourning, the woman also wore a very strange little round black hat and a black veil, which obscured her eyes. Aged in her late fifties or early sixties, the woman had wavy sandy hair curling from under her hat, and her thin lips were painted with heavy pink lipstick - as though she had put too much on.

"The moment I saw her I felt the hairs on the back of my neck go up. I said, 'Oh, you made me jump. I thought you were a ghost!'

"She wasn't wearing a visitor's badge, so I asked her if she was lost. The woman didn't speak. She just smiled strangely at me and then made an odd sighing sound. I felt so frightened that I turned and ran from her. Back in the call centre, I asked the remaining staff if any visitors were in the building. I was assured there were none. When I described what I had seen, they just laughed at me and told me I was imagining things. But I know what I saw."

The smartly-dressed ghost of a gentleman in a suit and waistcoat, carrying a briefcase, also roams the corridors at County Hall. Cleaners, office staff and a former hall-keeper have all reported sightings, and one day in 1995, former cleaner Sheila Etteridge noticed a man coming up the stone stairs from the basement level.

She explained, "My attention was drawn to him because he was not walking but gliding, and his feet made no sound on the steps. As I

These old buildings were demolished in 1967 to make way for County Hall's extension

looked at him, he stared back at me - then disappeared. That is when I knew I had seen a ghost. He wore a navy pin-stripe suit with a folded handkerchief in his breast pocket," recalled Sheila. "There was a terrible feeling of grief and unhappiness around him. When I described what I had seen to some of the other girls, they said that it was the spirit of a man who committed suicide some years ago haunting the building."

Sheila was often the target of a different, nosey and playful ghost. Although she never caught a glimpse of this one, she complained that doors opened and closed, lights flicked on and off, and telephones rang in rooms as she reached them, as if 'something' was following her around the building.

One of the Island's top hotels, the Swan Hotel, was adopted by the council as its first County Hall in 1919. The four-storey hotel was rebuilt in 1891 on the site of the former Swan Inn, dating from 1643. This in turn was

The Swan Hotel in 1891

demolished to make way for a new neo-Georgian County Hall, which opened in 1938. Thirty years later, the building was enlarged with a five-storey extension. During building work, no fewer than seven ancient brick and stone lined wells were discovered on the site. These were filled with concrete. The extension was built over the site of Hazards House, a fine old 17th century building which already had its own ghost; that of a maidservant who killed herself in a 'nasty dark cupboard' long ago. She was seen - and felt - by Newport business woman Audrey Spanner during the war. Audrey actually stepped aside and apologised to the apparition, which wore a long black skirt, when she bumped into her on the stairs. And curiously, many of County Hall's ghosts are still encountered on staircases.

MYSTERIOUS MUSLIN

There are many stories of ghosts taking or 'borrowing' a wide and often bizarre variety of objects. However, it is more unusual for new items to appear literally out of thin air. But that's what happened to a Newport family over a period of several months.

Julie Gabrielli and her husband live in Ash Road with twins Matthew and James, born in May 2004. Julie explained, "Early one morning, when the boys were about nine months old, I picked one of my sons up from his cot and noticed a small piece of white muslin cloth, about 2ins by 3ins, next to where he had been sleeping. I couldn't think where it had come from. My husband knew nothing either, so we forgot about it.

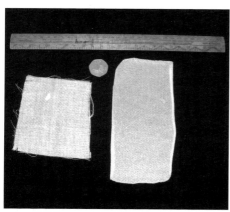

These squares of muslin appeared!

"A couple of months later, in April 2005, when I was unbuttoning one of the boys' sleepsuits, I found yet another square of muslin with torn edges, actually inside the sleepsuit. 'How on earth did that get there?' I asked my husband. We looked at the mattress sheet and checked both boys but found nothing else to match it with. How odd, we thought. On a third occasion, I found Matthew with another piece of muslin clutched in his tiny hand. On August 22nd 2006, I took both boys to their room for a sleep. Just before 12.30pm, I could hear them chattering to each other so I went to get them for lunch. As usual they had thrown all their toys onto the floor, and in the middle of them was yet another piece of cloth. I asked James, 'Where did that come from?' He pointed half way up the wall to an old built-in cupboard, but there were no muslin pieces inside. We can't understand where they are coming from."

Conversely, objects in the house have disappeared without trace. Baby toys have vanished from the bedroom, as have two new pairs of mittens bought for the twins.

Shortly after the couple moved into their house, which is about 100 years old, they noticed many odd smells. The very strong odour of Old Spice aftershave lingers on the upstairs landing, and a whole range of old-fashioned cooking smells occur in an area of the sitting room, directly under the twins' bedroom.

The delicious smells include steamed steak and kidney pudding, boiled gammon, and a roast dinner being cooked. More recently the family's taste buds were tickled by the strong, appetising aroma of coffee cake, which lingered a couple of minutes, one August morning.

"I'm sure there is nothing threatening here and the house has a warm, friendly feeling. I just wish I knew the significance of the muslin squares," said Julie. Three of the pieces were given to Judith, a Cowes psychic, to see what she could pick up from them. She believes they date from the 1920s. "At that time there were two children and a baby in the house. I feel that this is a happy, homely place and I have the impression that these pieces of material and appetising smells come from a cellular memory in the atmosphere and are a sign to say 'yes, we were happy here too' Judith said."

GHOST CALLS 'TIME' AT THE CASTLE INN

The Castle Inn situated in upper High Street is the oldest public house in Newport. Licensed since 1550, it was rebuilt after a fire in 1684. In ancient times the inn was within Castlehold, an area between St James's Square and Carisbrooke Road, which was a lawless and notorious haunt of criminals and ruffians, for the town constables and courts had no authority here. Only Carisbrooke Castle had jurisdiction and the Castle Inn's name originates here.

This historic hostelry, which was licensed by Royal warrant for cock fighting, boasts Royal connections, a secret passageway, and as befits a 17th century coaching inn, it also has a fine selection of beers, wines, spirits - and ghosts!

One is often up and about in the early hours of the morning. Many landlords have heard his peculiar tuneless whistle, usually between 2am and 3am, when the building is quiet. The eerie sound emanates from the old stables; for the ghostly whistler is said to be an ostler - a stable lad or groom - who hanged himself in the old hayloft in the 1600s. Research has shown that it was common in those days for stable lads to keep up this tuneless whistle in order to avoid inhaling the dust from hay and straw.

Former licensees Elizabeth and Steve Taylor quickly grew used to their ghosts' antics. One night when she was alone in the empty bar, Elizabeth saw a white shape enter through the locked front door then move slowly through the bar. The family's ginger cat often saw something, as did their dogs. Whenever the animals went up or down stairs, they would always walk carefully around an invisible obstruction at the halfway point. One of the pub ghosts also enjoyed watching television, and the Taylors often found the channels on the television in the bar kept changing.

Eddie Duff, another former licensee, confirmed that 'something' wanders around the empty pub at night. Once after midnight, an old staircase door creaked open - although it had been nailed shut. Old horse brasses stapled to a beam started to move and the pub clock jumped off the wall. Eddie often heard that phantom whistling between 2am and 3am. At first he would go downstairs to check, thinking there was someone in the old stable yard. It was always deserted.

After Sarah and Stuart Luke took over the pub in June 2004, they turned it into a traditional award-winning English inn once again, with panelled walls, flagstone floors, delicious food, ales, beers and wines ...and those ghosts. Supernatural activity at the Castle Inn continues unabated, with the month of June being an especially active time. All the ghosts are benign however, though their activities are often bizarre!

"The ghosts are very active here," said Sarah, who has taken to keeping a diary of paranormal activity at the pub. "Even as we were moving in, Stuart, who has always been a sceptic, came face to face with one in the back bedroom. He was here on his own and woke suddenly at 1am. There was a bright, full moon; he heard the creaking sound of someone moving about the room. Although it was a warm night, the

The Castle Inn is Newport's oldest - and most haunted - public house!

room felt very cold. There in the moonlight Stuart saw a shadowy, dark-featured Spanish-looking gentleman in heavy brocade clothes, dressed as if for winter. The man, who appeared to be in his thirties, seemed unaware of Stuart as he moved from one end of the room to the other, preceded by a strange 'swirly' shape with flecks of light.

"It was over in seconds. The swirly thing disappeared first, straight through the door, followed by the figure, then the extreme coldness. It was like someone was dragging a barrier of cold through the room. The temperature had dropped by over 10 degrees.

"On another occasion at between 2am and 3am, Stuart woke in our bedroom, to see a Cavalier standing in the corner of the room. He was looking towards the wall, which faces the High Street. The figure remained for a few seconds, then vanished."

Shortly afterwards, a woman who came in for lunch told Sarah, "I have just seen one of your ghosts. It was a Cavalier gentleman, with long hair and a moustache. I think he was a traveller, for he wore a long dark cloak which was spattered with mud."

A certain window in the old stable bar often opens on its own, sometimes several times in a night. The stable bar door closes on its own and, curiously, a ghost there likes to burst balloons. That room is often used for functions, and when balloons are put there for special celebrations they will burst, particularly when it's for a wedding, hen night, a girl's bash, or any event involving females. "I have seen at least 20 burst in there at a time. They will be popping around you as you are blowing them up," laughed Sarah. "It's like a child is having fun with them; even helium balloons deflate in there."

In the kitchen at the rear of the inn, pans have been observed moving on their own and a clock fastened securely to the wall frequently 'falls' off. Sometimes in the ladies' washroom, taps are turned fully on when the pub is closed and the hand drier, too, is found running. "This one's a clean ghost at least," said Sarah. Meanwhile in the men's washroom, startled customers are tapped on the shoulder by a ghostly hand.

The ghost's reward

One ghostly quirk Sarah enjoys is finding coins, which are left around the bar and staircase during the night. She frequently finds 5p pieces on the bar, the tables or floor, which have been deliberately placed there. "I have a big bag of 5p pieces now. At one time I was finding them there every day, but strangely, if I have been in a bad mood or irritable, I don't find any. It has become like a reward for me … and I am disappointed if no coins are there. Of course people drop other coins in the bar and restaurant during opening hours, but the ones I find in the morning are always 5p pieces."

More annoying is the way that keys in the bar disappear, while those problems with televisions and electrical equipment reported by former landlords, continue. The CD player in the bar turns itself on, blasting out at full volume, even when it is switched off after the bar is closed at night. Sarah's daughter, Abby, has watched the volume knob of her CD player being turned by an unseen hand, and when the family first moved in, she was often aware of 'someone' standing at the foot of her bed, at night, watching her. Barmaid Emma West, who saw this figure when she slept in Abby's room, awoke suddenly to find the ghost of a man peering at her.

"A lot of things happen when Emma is working; I think she is sensitive. I have felt and seen 'something' standing between me and the bar, and shortly afterwards Emma and I both watched a pen rise into the air and fall on the floor several feet away," said Sarah.

When customers have left and Stuart and Sarah are alone, they sometimes hear a loud hammering at the old front door. Then the door swings open, despite being locked and bolted. Door latches in the bar move up and down on their own, and in May 2007 one of the ghosts actually called 'time'. At 2am one morning, the couple who were in bed, heard the ship's bell on the bar ringing furiously. Stuart raced downstairs in time to see … nothing … except the bell rope swinging gently to and fro.

Lights in the bar are frequently switched on – usually between 2am and 3am, and if Stuart turns them off, they are on again when he comes down in the morning. Meanwhile in the cellar, Stuart occasionally senses 'someone' with him, and hears heavy footsteps when the cellar is empty. "We call this spirit 'Mr Angry' because he is so disruptive. He tips beer crates over, stomps around at night and throws packets of crisps about," Stuart said.

A team from Midland Paranormal heard and recorded these footsteps, during overnight investigations at the Castle Inn in 2005 and 2006. On both occasions, sounds were recorded in the empty premises and investigator Mark Cave heard a ghost cat meowing in the empty bar.

During their first visit in 2005, digital recording equipment which was locked in the cellar picked up sounds of heavy wooden items being moved around while whistling and voices talking are heard in the background. In the bar and restaurant area a small, dark shapeless shadow was seen moving between the fireplace and restaurant. Members investigating the washroom area heard a loud bang from the locked cellars, which also registered on recording equipment.

An extract from the investigation report on 26 October 2006:

02:13: Investigators heard movement in the bar area of wooden
      furniture, a chair or stool, moving on the flagstone floor

02:15: A wooden chair or stool was heard moving in the bar

02:39: Furniture was heard moving in the bar

03:03: Investigators heard a catch on the front door being operated. No
      one was there. Both the main entrance door and the old staircase
      doorway were locked

Investigation of stable bar

04:11: Footsteps were heard in the middle of the room at the back,
      sounding like bare feet on stone (the stable now has a wooden

floor) footsteps moved towards and past the investigators

04:32: Light footsteps like those of a child, were heard on the left side of the stable bar six feet away from investigators

04:46: The sound of door hinges and a door opening was heard

Investigation of bar & restaurant

05:25: Movement of furniture heard

05:40: A grunt, like someone clearing their throat, was heard about six feet from the investigators

05:46: The sound of furniture moving in the restaurant was heard

On September 25th 2005, during an all night vigil with Marc Tuckey's Paranormal Perambulations team, medium Chris located several spirits at the inn, including an elderly man named William, who haunts the bar area, is apparently happy to remain in the pub and tries his best to be seen. Chris said, "There is a lady here who lost a child. She walks up and down stairs looking for him and often stands by the fireplace. Walter, a young boy aged six or seven years is here on his own. He is nothing to do with this lady, but she looks after him. He is very pale and died of an illness.

"Whoever haunts the Gents is angry. This spirit moves through walls to the cellar and is furious because his life was taken here in 1807. He was killed by a blow to head with something wooden, possibly a club. His name is Robert or Robin and he is connected with the sea. The inn was once possibly a brothel and 'ladies of the night' worked here."

Given the lawless nature of Castlehold and its proximity to the aptly-named Paradise Row (now Castlehold Lane) this is highly likely.

The spirit of a stable 'lad' aged about 35 confirmed to Chris that he had hanged himself from a beam in the stables in March 1751 and that he has visited Abby upstairs. Curiously, three people on the vigil found 5p coins in their pockets after leaving the cellar.

Medium Leslie George of Cowes agrees the Castle Inn is full of spirits. "There is an immense amount of activity here," he told Sarah and Stuart during a visit one Saturday afternoon in June 2007. Les described the hunched, thickset figure of a man with long, straggly grey hair, who haunts the rear of the restaurant and kitchen area. "He has been here a very long time, as long as the building. He means no harm and cannot hurt anyone.

"Another spirit here is a previous owner or landlord. He's completely at home and can move wherever he likes. He wears a dark suit and cap and is an important man in the town. I think he is the one deliberately placing those 5p coins for Sarah as a sign of approval and reward." (For some 80 years from the 1860s to the 1940s, the Mursell family were landlords at the Castle Inn. Is one of them leaving the 5p coins?)

Les received strong images of a cheerful couple who, he feels, came from a farm at Whitecroft. "The landlord here was kind to them and gave them crusts, scraps, and the odd drink. They were devoted to each other in life. They died together and in death are still in love and inseparable. He wears a coarse, white top and baggy trousers tied up with string. His feet are bare. She is behind him laughing. They love playing jokes and muck around downstairs moving things; they are simple souls. He is so proud of her and keeps saying 'She's my May!' in a broad Isle of Wight accent."

This photograph of the stableboy's 'hanging ghost' was taken in the Stable Bar at 11.42pm on June 4th 2006. In honour of this ghost, a special beer, 'The Stableboy's Revenge' brewed at the (haunted) Ventnor Brewery, is now on sale at The Castle Inn.

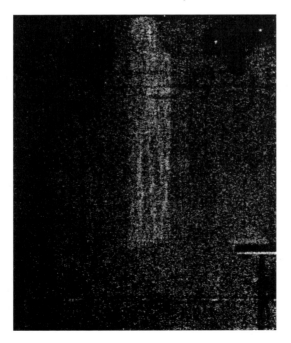

Visit the Castle Inn at: *www.thecastleiow.co.uk*

One of 'Palmerston's Follies', Spitbank Fort in the Solent, is haunted by the ghost of a soldier who was killed in an explosion there in 1910. The four Solent forts were nicknamed after Prime Minister Lord Palmerston, who began his political career as Member of Parliament for Newport in 1807. Spitbank Fort was originally painted in this distinctive chequered pattern as a navigational aid to shipping.

Visit Spitbank Fort at: www.spitbankfort.co.uk

Chapter Eight

GHOST SOLDIERS AND HAUNTED FORTS

The Isle of Wight has long been a vital strategic point for invading forces looking for a bridgehead into mainland Britain. A defence network to resist them still stands - from the Spithead forts in the eastern Solent to the Needles Battery, Golden Hill Fort and Fort Redoubt guarding the western approaches. Although all are now decommissioned, not all the soldiers have left. Their ghosts live on…

GHOST AT SPITBANK FORT

For well over a century, four massive granite sea fortresses have guarded the Solent approaches to Portsmouth and the Isle of Wight. Nicknamed Palmerston's Follies, after the Prime Minister who authorised their construction, they were intended to guard Britain from the threat of French invasion, but never fired a gun in anger.

Spitbank Fort, the smallest of the four, took 16 years to build, and was manned by 150 men. Completed in 1878, it is 162ft in diameter and its 15ft thick, armour-plated granite walls have withstood the waves for over 100 years. After it was declared surplus to military requirements in 1962, a local businessman bought the fort from the Ministry of Defence and opened it to the public in 1984.

This famous Solent landmark has over 50 rooms and a maze of passages, massive basements and 35ft of solid stone foundations with a fresh water artesian well, capable of pumping 23,000 gallons of water a day. Visitors can see the original layout of the fort, including the gunroom, and enjoy spectacular views across the Solent.

In 2005, a consortium of Hampshire businessmen bought the Grade II listed Ancient Monument as a unique entertainment centre.

So when young Thomas Abbott of Staplehurst Grange, Newport, went there during his school activities week in 2007, he and his friends were excited at the prospect of exploring the massive fortress. Thomas explains, "After we looked around and had our lunch, we were allowed to go into the basement to explore. There were three of us; two of my mates went to the left but I went to the right. It was quite dark down there and I was on my own. Suddenly I saw this man come out of the stone wall about five feet in front of me. I was petrified.

"The man looked solid and real. He had dark hair, black clothes and was aged about thirty. We stood and looked at one another for what seemed like ages. He didn't speak. Then he moved forward into another stone wall and disappeared. I did not believe in ghosts before. I do now!"

Island-born Pauline Horsham, now living in Gosport, has also seen the fort ghost. Pauline who has worked at Spitbank since 2001, has often been there alone at night, and has glimpsed the shadowy figure known by staff as Henry – the name of the only soldier known to have died on active service at the fort. He was apparently cleaning out one of the guns when a shell became stuck, backfired, and blew him apart.

The Times newspaper dated August 16th 1910, reported: *The funeral of Sergeant Henry Attrill, of the 67th Company of Royal Garrison Artillery, who lost his life by the gun explosion at the Spitbank Fort on Thursday last, took place with full military honours at the Highland Road Cemetery, Portsmouth. All the principal officers of the Royal Garrison Artillery in the town also attended, as well as about 500 non-commissioned officers and men.*

Pauline said, "I have been out there in all weathers; you either love or hate the place. I think it is wonderful. This is the best job in the world. I have never felt really frightened or threatened there, although I have seen the dark shadow moving about the place and I always call out 'Hello Henry' when I sense him around. Sometimes when I'm on my own, I hear my name being called. It's a man's voice saying 'Oh, Pauline'.

"I think he was a smoker because, sometimes of an evening, I smell strong, old-fashioned cigarette smoke in the air, like an old Players Navy Cut. One night in the summer of 2006, I was on the roof when I suddenly smelled the strong perfume of flowers. It was a lovely, if unexpected smell, just one of those odd things that happen at Spitbank Fort.

"During the celebrations for the 200th anniversary of the Battle of Trafalgar, we were astonished to see a stall we had set up in the courtyard being thrown across the floor. I'm positive it was Henry letting us know he was there!

"One night I had to check the basement when visitors had left. Unusually I was reluctant to go on my own and when I finally plucked up courage to go, I was halfway round the corridor when I felt something – or someone – blow in my ear. I actually felt breath on my face and my hair flew up. Since that night I haven't gone into the basement on my own."

GHOSTLY SOLDIERS AT THE ZOO

Originally it was designed to repel visitors, now it seeks to attract them. However, the Isle of Wight Zoo cannot escape its military past. Although no shot was ever fired in anger from its granite walls, a young soldier was cut in half in an horrific accident at old Sandown Fort, which

now houses the world-renowned zoo. Since his agonising death, this soldier's ghost has been seen by keepers and staff over many years.

The fort was built between 1861 and 1864 to defend against French invasion, but the four officers and 67 men stationed there never saw action. It was eventually decommissioned and sold in 1930. Today, the privately owned zoo, which was first opened as Sandown Zoo in 1955 by Ron and Betty Bateman, is an established centre for wild animal management and conservation programmes

Now the Isle of Wight Zoo, old Sandown Fort can be seen in the foreground of this photograph from the 1950s

housing tigers, lions, lemurs and other endangered species. Its mission now is to promote the survival of endangered species through educational and recreational experiences, conservation and research.

In 1976, the late Jack Corney took over the then failing zoo, and after hearing tales of the soldier's ghost from keepers and staff, he located an inquest report into the tragedy from 1888. He discovered that the fort's Victorian guns were massive and, when fired, the recoil was absorbed by the wheeled mounts they rested upon. The accident occurred when a number of soldiers were carrying out maintenance on them. The rope holding a gun barrel slipped. As the 18-ton gun rolled backwards, the sergeant jumped clear, shouting a warning to the soldier working under the gun. But it was too late. The wretched man was caught halfway out. The heavy gun slid backwards cutting him in half.

In the century since then, his ghost - among others - has been seen in the fort. 'Something' tampers with the electric lights in the old fort tunnels, and staff have reported a very spooky feeling there at times, especially near the old gun emplacement.

General manager Greg Hailes was very sceptical about the ghost stories until he accompanied a group of ghost-hunters on a vigil there one summer night in 2006, and was stroked by a ghostly hand.

Greg recalls, "It was about 1am and three of us were sitting against a wall in the end room of the old fort. My torch was misbehaving and kept turning itself off and on; then it wouldn't work at all. One of the video cameras went dead as well. I began to feel nauseous and quite unwell. Sitting there, I distinctly felt someone stroke my hair, then two fingers prodded me in the middle of my back. Both these things were impossible, because I was sitting against the wall!"

The earlier Sandham Fort or Castle, built by Henry VIII in 1537, was also the scene of a tragedy when a master gunner went insane. He shot his wife and child, and after threatening to blow up the fort, cut his own throat. But the self-inflicted injury was not fatal, and he was still able to put himself under arrest.

Visit the zoo at: *www.isleofwightzoo.co.uk*

'I was petrified'

Few people would live in a caravan among lions, panthers and leopards. But for Janet Fisher it went with the job, and from 1967 to 1969, she lived *inside* Sandown Zoo. Now retired, Janet has fond memories of her time at the zoo when she and her partner, Nick, (the head-keeper 'Nyoka') owned Simba the lion, Zebeddee the puma, four leopards, two black panthers and several assorted snakes. "During the winters, it was just Nick and me in the caravan. The zoo was closed to the public out of season, but we lived on site to look after our animals. We were caged there - like them," said Janet. "They were great years and we really had such fun. We took the big cats out for regular walks along the beach at Sandown. They absolutely loved it."

Janet knew nothing of the zoo's reputation for being haunted until she stayed there on her own when Nick was away. "I used to hate being on my own at night in that

Out for a morning walk on Sandown beach!

caravan. There were the odd noises from the animals of course, but sometimes I heard other sounds in the night; men's voices and footsteps running. However I could never make out what the voices were saying - or where they came from.

"There was an area at the back of the zoo where the foodstuff for the animals was kept. It was like an archway with a huge drop underneath that led to the underground chambers and rooms. Most of the noises seemed to come from there. It was known by staff as 'round the back' and it had a very unpleasant feeling. It was nothing you could put your finger on, but I felt very uneasy there, as though I was being watched."

One summer's evening, Janet finally glimpsed those soldiers on ghostly manoeuvres. "One of my jobs was to climb onto the walls to raise the flags in the morning and take them down at night. One night the gates were locked and I was alone in the zoo. I had lowered the flags and was about to climb down when I heard the sound of heavy boots on the stones beneath. There below me were several soldiers in uniform. I only caught a glimpse of the figures so I couldn't tell what era they were from, but I continued to hear those marching feet for several minutes.

"I was petrified and it was at least three hours before I dared venture back down and then I shot into the caravan, locking the door. That was the only time I actually saw the ghosts. I don't know if the big cats ever sensed anything there. I know domestic cats will sometimes stare intently at something unseen, so perhaps lions and leopards see spirits too!"

GHOSTS AT GOLDEN HILL

Set on top of a hill where it can be seen for miles is Golden Hill Fort at Freshwater, a Grade I Listed Building and Scheduled Ancient Monument. Another link in the chain of defensive fortresses, this two-storey building with a central courtyard is approached through a tunnel across a moat. Built between 1863 and 1872 at a cost of £38,000, the six-sided brick barracks once housed 128 men and eight officers. Its guns, which never fired in anger, were intended to cover the coastal batteries from attack by the French. Millions of bricks were used in its construction and three underground escape tunnels led from the fort.

Once there were married quarters within the fort, and the ghostly sound of children's voices can still be heard when everything is quiet. The distinctive aroma of old-fashioned pipe tobacco also lingers within the walls and is often smelled at the top of the circular stone staircase.

After being decommissioned, the fort enjoyed a chequered history as a craft and business park, with a small museum and nightclub. Many initiatives there failed. Vandalism and fire accelerated the fort's decline and it was placed on the Buildings at Risk Register. In 2005, permission was granted to convert the building into seventeen three and four-bedroom town houses and one flat, for a conglomerate of individuals acting as a self-build group.

Pushed to his death?

When Ivor and Jill Allison lived at Golden Hill in the 1980s, the fort was almost derelict. As managers, they became familiar with its maze of winding corridors and arched rooms, often welcoming back ex-servicemen who were once stationed there. Military graffiti, names, regiments and dates can still be seen carved deep into the brickwork around the fort. They also became familiar with the fort's ghosts, one of whom smoked a very sweet aromatic pipe, whose aroma lingered in the corridor near their office in early mornings or late at night.

Unsuspecting visitors often asked why there were servicemen in old-fashioned uniforms about the fort. One sailor was often seen lounging in a doorway smoking his pipe. Those once stationed at Golden Hill included men from the Royal Artillery, Isle of Wight Rifles, the Royal Hampshires and Royal Militia of Jersey. A sergeant-major from one of these regiments fell (or was pushed!) to his death during the First World War. Hated by his men, he plunged down one of the fort's stone spiral

Haunted Golden Hill Fort at Freshwater was formerly used as light industrial units

staircases, breaking his neck. The 'accident' was hushed up; official reports stated he was 'killed in action'. His uniformed ghost has been seen on the roof and in the old officers' mess. His fellow-phantom is a 19th century sailor, one of a small number of naval ratings stationed at Golden Hill. He, it is whispered, attempted to sell plans of the fort's defences to the French. For his treason he was condemned to death and spent his last hours before execution in the fort's cells.

Ghost in a temper

When he moved into the fort in 1998 to run the museum, Ben Cunliffe, now an archivist in Staffordshire, soon discovered its haunted reputation. At that time, it was owned by a leisure company, which was turning part of the fort into a nightclub.

"It wasn't long before staff told me of strange things they had seen and heard. One Friday night, a staff member saw a figure moving about in locked rooms above the pub and café. On another occasion, the resident DJ had just opened the pub when he heard the door open and slam shut with considerable force, as if someone was in a temper. He hurried to the bar to see who had come in, but the bar was empty. Then he heard footsteps behind him. Whirling around, he was shocked to find himself alone. Another night, the inner door leading from the pub to the moat outside started to shake violently as if someone was trying to get in - an impossibility - for the outer door was locked and bolted."

Ben was busy in the museum workshop one evening when, as he watched in disbelief, a small electric organ was flipped into the air, landing on the floor with a crash. At the same time the resident DJ, working in a small studio across the corridor, experienced an electrical surge, which sent his equipment haywire.

"The smell of aromatic pipe smoke was a regular occurrence around the old fort. A visitor to the director's apartment smelled 'old men's tobacco' one evening in the living area, and later as she walked down the stairs from the kitchen in the empty fort, she was so startled to see a ghostly man's figure emerge from the laundry room that she dropped the glass she was holding.

"A team of paranormal investigators who set up a camera overnight in a part of the fort known as the Victorian corridor, captured the hazy image of a figure carrying a bucket, standing in a doorway in what appeared to be naval uniform. Unfortunately I don't know what happened to that photograph," said Ben regretfully.

Do ghosts still walk here at Golden Hill Fort?

"There was a strange atmosphere in the place. We ran some occasional spooky ghostwalks there, which were very popular with visitors. However, most of the shops and units had closed, so we ended up with the museum in a mostly unoccupied building. After I left, I think some exhibits disappeared and it was vandalised. It is odd just how many things failed there."

Chapter Nine

SPIRITS OF VENTNOR BOTANIC GARDENS

Today, Ventnor Botanic Gardens with its 22 acres of landscaped gardens is a beautiful and tranquil place for visitors and Islanders alike. It is also one of the most haunted places on the Isle of Wight! Gardeners and ghost-hunters alike are attracted to the gardens, but for very different reasons. By day, they come to enjoy the magnificent plants, shrubs and trees. By night, supernatural seekers come to explore the gardens' darker side on ghost walks and vigils. Countless stories of ghosts, hauntings and paranormal activity have been reported there. Here are but a few...

THE HOSPITAL REFUSED TO DIE

For almost a century the Royal National Hospital at Ventnor was at the forefront of the fight against tuberculosis. Some 100,000 patients were treated here. Many were cured, some weren't so fortunate. Much pioneering and experimental surgery was carried out in the operating theatre, but until the arrival of new and effective drugs in the 1950s, consumption remained a highly infectious killer.

When the last patient left in May 1964, the hospital doors were ceremonially locked. For the next five years the buildings and grounds became a derelict wilderness. In 1969, the eleven blocks of balconied cottages, stretching for almost half-a-mile, were demolished. Then like a phoenix from the ashes, Ventnor Botanic Gardens rose from the ruins.

But the old hospital did not go quietly. Its death throes brought ghost hunters and psychic investigators from all over the world. For the hospital was haunted. Supernatural activity centred around the old operating theatre. The last part of the building to be torn down, it resisted all efforts at demolition. Four tractors, excavators and a ball crane were wrecked in the attempt. The operating theatre was still standing while the rest of the hospital was reduced to rubble.

Roy Dore of St Lawrence was curator at the time of the demolition in 1969. Roy who worked for Ventnor Urban District Council, which bought the 33-acre site from the Ministry of Health, recalled what a headache the operating theatre caused for Gosport demolition contractors, Treloar and Sons. "They tried to knock it down with a crane

The old Royal National Hospital at Ventnor was more than half a mile in length

and ball, but the steel cable snapped. Then they brought in a large tracked tractor. Three huge pieces of masonry fell on it, crushing the cab, smashing the transmission and breaking the steel tracks. A small caterpillar tractor with a steel hawser was used to pull the walls down, but the hook and cable attachment on the back snapped right off. Another caterpillar tractor became entangled with the broken cable from the first attempt and at that point they gave up."

Long after the rest of the hospital was just a pile of bricks, the operating theatre held out. Ether could still be smelled and Roy was among those who noticed it. Workmen talked openly of ghosts. Two men, told to demolish the operating theatre with sledgehammers, were confronted by a ghostly figure standing in a doorway.

Another patient appears...

Those empty hospital buildings were like a magnet for young Freddy Morris and his friends. "In 1966-7 when we were 12 and 13 years old, we would go there to 'explore' after school. The place was empty, and we would go into the old wards and the abandoned operating theatre too. One afternoon we were messing around near the boiler room and one of the old open wards (now the potting shed) when a gentleman appeared in front of us.

"He was in his late twenties or early thirties and wore a very thick woollen, blue and red checked dressing gown with a red collar and a silk cord tied around his waist. He had carpet slippers on his feet.

"The man asked what we were doing there. He was very softly spoken but his voice gave me goose pimples. We didn't hang about, we all ran and when we got back to the road, we just looked at one another. As we discussed what had happened, it became apparent that two of the lads with us hadn't seen anyone. They only ran because we did! That was when we realised we had just seen a ghost.

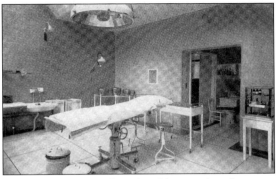

Ghosts were seen when the old operating theatre was finally demolished by workmen

"I don't think any of us was brave enough to go there again. When you were in the old wards you would have the distinct feeling of being watched and you would occasionally hear a soft cough or movement. Before we saw the ghost we had put this down to the other kids, as it wasn't unusual to try to frighten other 'gangs' playing there.

"The place had a strange atmosphere, which wasn't surprising, given its past. The areas near the old operating theatre, the old tunnel to the cliff and the present potting shed, where I saw the man in the dressing gown, were the worst. I remember we had just been inside the shed, rooting around in the rubbish and old bed frames for 'treasures' when we met him."

It pulled my hair

Lucie Evans and three friends visited the gardens one summer's night in 2003. It was a very warm night, clear and still with no breeze. Lucie, who is used to seeing spirits, explained, "Since my first visit to the botanic gardens at the age of nine, I've had some rather strange experiences there. When

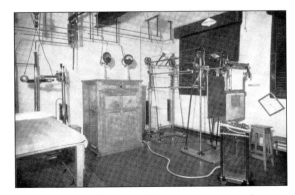

The old hopital's state of the art x-ray room!

I am there I always feel nervous and on edge and sense someone with me. That night I was apprehensive because I had never visited after dark and was reluctant to 'disturb' whatever walks there.

"As we sat by the pond at about 11pm, I felt my hair being gently pulled from out of my pony tail. I was so aware of this feeling that I wanted to leave. As we walked back to the car park I could feel I was being followed very closely … but the feeling wasn't a nice one. As I tried to hurry my friends, we got lost. All the time that malevolent feeling was growing stronger, as though 'something' didn't want me there any more. That sensation didn't ease until we reached the car park.

"Since then I have been asked many times to go back but have refused. I also discovered that one of my friends sitting on the bench with me had felt her hair being pulled as well that night."

A DARK ENTITY

Every year many hundreds of people enjoy ghost walks at the botanic gardens, led by Marc Tuckey of Paranormal Perambulations. Ghostwalk team member, Ross Kirk, had spent many nights lurking in the dark gardens ready to scare unwary ghost walkers, but when he agreed to take three friends around the gardens one New Year's Day, he hadn't expected to meet a ghost himself!

Ross admitted, "It was about 2am on January 1st 2006 and all of us, except the driver, had had a drink or two. They wanted me to take them somewhere scary, so I suggested the botanic gardens. It was a very atmospheric, damp and misty night so I didn't tell any of the stories, I just led them round the ghostwalk route. When we reached the path to Steephill Cove, I noticed someone standing on the cliff top.

"I shouted, 'Can I help you?' Suddenly the figure moved so quickly that it blurred and vanished. As I led my friends to the car park, I looked back. I glimpsed something black move behind a bush. Whatever this was, it wasn't human. The figure was very tall with extremely long thin, spindly arms and legs. It crouched, as if hiding, behind the large shrub. I have never before felt afraid to be at the botanic gardens, but I did then. I remember thinking, I want to leave, NOW!

"My friends saw me staring at the bush and asked what the matter was. I laughed it off and quickly got them into the car and shut the doors. One of them, Gemma, said in a low voice, 'You saw it, didn't you?' I asked what she meant. She told me she had seen a black haze,

As part of their therapy patients were expected to work in the hospital grounds

like dark smoke, moving behind the bush and had a bad feeling about it."

By the following July when Marc and the team, including a medium, spent an overnight vigil at Ventnor Botanic Gardens, Ross had almost persuaded himself that he had imagined that figure. "It was another of those damp, overcast nights. At about 2am, we were just off the main path, south of the visitor centre, when the medium, who was leading a group of thirty people, made a panicky sound and stopped so suddenly that they almost collided with one another. Marc sent me forward to see what had happened.

"The medium was agitated and muttered, 'The speed of it. I have never seen anything like this before'. He was unable to carry on, so we called a break and went indoors for refreshments. The medium was trembling so badly that his cup was quivering! He said the entity he had seen wasn't human."

Remembering the odd figure he had seen, Ross asked the medium what had frightened him. His description of a dark being with a squat body and long, thin arms and legs sounded horribly familiar, although he never told anyone else what he had seen that New Year's Day.

Confirmation of the strange encounter came from someone who had been next to the medium at the front of the group. "This chap was shocked to have seen what he described as a black misty or smoky shape, like a dark miasma in the air which suddenly moved at high speed. The medium was reluctant to go back outside, but I wasn't going to be frightened off and wanted to investigate further, so I took him to where I had seen the figure on the cliff top and asked, 'Are you picking up anything here?'

"All he said was, 'It's still around. It's always here and it moves through the trees.' That gave me quite a turn," said Ross.

The smuggler's spirit

Long before the hospital was built on the clifftop site, this sparsely populated area of the Undercliff at St Lawrence was a smugglers' haven. In centuries past, ruthless smuggling gangs brought contraband ashore at lonely landings like Steephill Cove. Indeed, until 2005, the Island's Museum of Smuggling History illustrating over 700 years of smuggling practices was housed in old underground galleries at the botanic gardens. Even today smuggling gangs still use the area; in 2002 eight smugglers were jailed for a total of 141 years when they were caught with £90 million worth of cocaine at nearby Woody Bay.

So was it coincidence that when Cowes medium Leslie George visited the gardens in May 2007, he encountered the larger than life spirit of a smuggler not far from the visitor centre on a path leading to Steephill Cove? "His name is Michael but he is known as Pierre - because he trades with the French. This spirit is not aware he is dead. I am not shown how he died, but I think his was a violent death and that he died somewhere else, not here. But this place was important to him, that's why he is still here.

"Pierre is a very muscular chap, over six feet tall. He's tough and not afraid of anyone. He was around in the early 17th century. He is clean-shaven, with a mop of blond curly hair. He doesn't wear a hat. He has dark trousers, a light top and high leather boots turned over at the top. Although Pierre is a happy-go-lucky character, he is definitely the 'top man' and what he says goes."

Les may have an answer to the ghostly goings-on at the potting shed too, for as he paused there, he was poked in the back by the spirit of an elderly man who worked as a gardener at the hospital in the early 20th century. "I think he was trying to attract my attention," said Les. "This man has a spinal problem, he is bent right over and walks with a stoop. I feel he is in a lot of pain. He has a beard, gingery whiskers, and wears baggy trousers with wide turn-ups and a shabby jacket. This is 'his' part of the gardens and he takes an interest in everything that happens here." Read more haunting stories here in *The Original Ghosts of the Isle of Wight*.

Chapter Ten

GHOSTS OF ARRETON

APPARITIONS AT ARRETON MANOR

Ancient Arreton Manor abounds with ghosts. A figure in silvery-grey is associated with the overpowering fragrance of spring flowers. Also accompanied by the scents of spring is the ghost of a woman in a tight-waisted, puff-sleeved dress of deep cherry red - a woman with long, curly black hair, whose face is never seen. The occasional phantom monks and smells of incense there come from a time when Arreton Manor belonged to the Abbey of Quarr.

A brutal family murder lies behind the most persistent of the many hauntings here. Local legend tells that when wealthy landowner Barnaby Leigh lay sick in his bed, his son John, keen for his inheritance, smothered him with a pillow. Annabelle, John's little sister, saw the dreadful deed. He dragged her, screaming, into an upstairs room, where an area of coldness can be felt today, and pushed her through the window to her death.

Annabelle is often seen around the house and gardens. She wears a long blue dress, white slippers laced with ribbon, and her hair falls in tight blonde curls. Her cry of 'Mamma, mamma' has a pitiful air.

Set in five acres of land, nestled in Arreton Downs, three miles from Newport, the manor was mentioned in Alfred the Great's will in 885AD. The present manor, an early Jacobean house, still possesses many Tudor features - and a secret passage. During his exile from London, King Charles I stayed at the manor and a hidden room was built for him in the west bedroom, where the entrance still exists.

Apart from such sounds as the grave chanting of monks, footsteps, the rustle of a skirt and Annabelle's voice, the late Leslie Slade (known as Count Slade de Pomeroy) who owned and lived at the manor with his wife and family for 25 years, was often woken by mysterious rappings on his bedroom door. No one was ever there. When the Slades left, the manor ghosts seemed disturbed and staff complained that spectral monks haunting the tearooms were becoming particularly bothersome.

After further changes in ownership, during which it was closed to the public for some years, Arreton Manor became the family home of Andy

Ghosts abound at ancient Arreton Manor, pictured here in August 2007

and Julia Gray-Ling and their children, Amie and Will. They have re-opened the manor and guests can now stay overnight in luxurious four-poster splendour. Andy has worked tirelessly on the manor's tranquil grounds, building terraces and planting a Tudor-style knot garden.

"It is such a special house with a fascinating history and it is because of this that we open up our home to share with the public at certain times of the year, for all to enjoy," said Julia.

The ghosts evidently approve, for they are still very much around. Occasionally the smell of pungent old-fashioned tobacco smoke appears from nowhere, a lame ghost with a stick or crutch is heard tap-tapping his way upstairs, and friends of the family staying in the west bedroom with its carved four-poster bed, were startled one night to see a dark haired woman in a white shift glide across the room and vanish straight through the window....

'Most Haunted' visit

A loud knocking is heard at the heavy wooden front door when no one is there. And when Living TV's 'Most Haunted' programme visited Arreton Manor in January 2005, several ghosts made their presence known, including one which flung a book across the Great Hall. This manifestation was caught on film, and the book - appropriately - was a copy of *The Original Ghosts of the Isle of Wight*, which features stories of the ghosts of Arreton Manor.

You can visit the manor at: *www.arretonmanor.co.uk*

Annabelle appears

Little Annabelle actually spoke to Andy's father Jack, one night, when she walked into his room in the west wing at the rear of the house, and stood at the foot of the bed.

Jack explains, "I always leave the bedroom door open, and that night, something woke me. Looking towards the door I saw a young girl with blonde hair and what I took to be a long, blue nightdress, gliding towards me. I didn't have my glasses on, so thinking it was my granddaughter, Amie, I called out 'hello'. The little girl replied, 'hello', then she ducked down by the side of the bed, and disappeared.

"I woke my wife and said 'Amie is in here and needs taking back to bed.' But when we looked, the room was empty and we found Amie fast asleep in her own bed. That's when I realised I had seen, and spoken with, Annabelle's little ghost.

"It was a very serene, almost peaceful experience. It's hard to explain, but it was as though she was in a vacuum. I was awake and I know I did not dream it. I still remember her voice so clearly. It was such a sweet little voice."

Spirit on a horse

Little Annabelle's ghost wasn't around the afternoon that Cowes medium Leslie George visited the manor in May 2007, but the overbearing spirit of a horseman certainly was. Sitting quietly in the warm afternoon sun, Les was soon conscious of this man's spirit riding up to the front door on a large chestnut horse.

Living history groups often visit Arreton Manor

"Two grooms hurry forward to hold the horse's bridle as the visitor dismounts and strides into the house. He is a very important man connected with the military, and exudes an aura of authority and power, although he is not the owner of the manor. He is titled; he is 'Sir' something. He's in his mid to late forties and is wearing riding boots, breeches and a white, full-sleeved shirt. He has a shiny leather belt with a scabbard and a narrow-bladed sword. I don't see a hat, but he has a bald patch on top and long hair hanging down over his collar.

"I get this picture over and over again; it keeps replaying in front of me. This energy is so very strong and I have the impression that he is connected with the Royalists and King Charles. There is a lot of spirit activity going on here at Arreton Manor …"

Through the secret door …

When former Islander Liz Bradshaw of Sheffield visited the manor with her family in August 2006, she knew its reputation for being haunted, but didn't expect to see or experience anything herself.

"The guide had taken us through that 'secret' door and onto the landing which leads down to the cellars. As she was talking about the monks who once lived at the manor, I began to feel the most awful pressure in my stomach, as if I'd been winded. I started to feel faint and breathless; it's hard to describe, but it was as I imagine it would feel to be stabbed. Noticing my discomfort, the guide asked if I was alright, as I had apparently cried out with the pain. When I told her what had happened, she said that another visitor had also experienced the same sensation on that same spot.

"Another odd thing happened to my 17-year-old daughter. She was waiting beneath an old tree in the gardens while we finished in the tearooms. Suddenly she was struck on the back by a tiny missile like a stone. She thought at first it was a child's prank, but she was alone and there were not any nuts or fruit on that tree - nor any squirrels! Was little Annabelle having some fun with her?"

SPIRIT ON A SECRET STAIRCASE

As a boy, Barry Pike grew up in the shadow of Arreton Manor. His family lived opposite the village church in Stile House, one of the oldest farmhouses on the Island. Now settled near Apse Manor, Shanklin, Barry has spent many years building and restoring properties.

Arreton Manor is pictured here in 1905, at the turn of the twentieth century

"My family was closely involved with the manor in the 1940s and 50s. My father and grandmother both worked for Charles Buckett Yates who owned the manor and surrounding farms. Father, who worked on the farm, was gardener at the manor and also chauffeured Mr Yates around. Grandmother was a housekeeper and would sleep in, taking care of the house when Mr Yates was away - for he would never leave the house unattended.

"One day when I was ten, I heard grandmother telling my uncle about the 'friendly ghost' at the manor which, she insisted, often moved through her room at 10pm. Of course I wanted to see this for myself, so the next time grandmother stayed at the manor, I went with her. Her room, which was in the west wing on the first floor, was panelled from floor to ceiling in oak. A curious 'cropped' corner to the left of the fireplace was also panelled and no one knew what lay behind it.

"At 9.30pm I went to bed on an old army camp bed in front of the fireplace and fell into a light sleep. Suddenly, at 10pm I was wide-awake. I could hear 'something' approaching from that boxed-in corner. It wasn't completely dark so I could still see around the room. But though I could hear and sense a warm presence moving around, I couldn't see anything. I physically felt a warm glow from an incredibly friendly, calming presence, as it moved slowly across the room, out of the door and down the stairs. I didn't hear footsteps, but was aware of the old wooden floorboards creaking gently as the ghost moved over them.

"I experienced the whole thing twice, for a few nights later I slept in that room again. Once more the sounds started within the boxed-in corner, moved across the room, down the stairs, and to the door of the 'secret' passage."

When Barry told his grandmother, she just smiled and said, 'I told you so, didn't I?'

Some years later, when the Slade family bought the manor, they removed rotting wooden boards from a wall near the kitchens downstairs. Hidden behind they discovered an old wooden spiral staircase covered in dust and cobwebs. The top of these long-forgotten stairs emerged behind that boarded-in corner in the bedroom where the warm presence was felt. For Barry everything suddenly fell into place. The 'friendly ghost' had come up that spiral staircase into the bedroom, before walking through the room and back down the main stairs!

Figures in the moonlight

From his bedroom window at Stile House, which overlooks the graveyard of St George's Church, young Barry saw more of Arreton's ghosts. "It always happened on moonlit nights; I would wake suddenly in the middle of the night and get up to look out of the window. I never

knew what had woken me, but I would see four or five hooded figures milling around near the graves. They were always silent. I never saw their faces but I know I was not dreaming. I even pinched myself to make sure!

This old painting shows Stile House and Arreton Church

"I would watch them for several minutes until they started to somehow go 'out of focus' and vanish, one by one. It was so weird. I saw those figures on several occasions, and the next morning I always went into the churchyard to see if the grass had been flattened or trodden down. It never was."

Could these be the same apparitions seen one moonlit night in the 1950s by sisters Joan and Betty Eldridge and their neighbours? The tall, hooded figures were observed standing motionless on the path to the church.

They wore dark mourning coats with plain white clerical collars. Their featureless faces were smooth and lifeless, as though made of marble or wax and their eyes were closed. (Read this story in *Ghosts of the Isle of Wight Book IV*)

ON GALLOWS HILL

On Gallows Hill and in nearby Burnt House Lane, the ghost of a woodsman carrying an axe still walks. Over the years, the restless spirit of murderous woodcutter Michael Morey, has been seen there several times. Morey was executed for the killing of his young grandson, 14-year-old James Dove, in cold blood The trial at Winchester Assizes in 1737 heard the boy was killed with a billhook which Morey then used to cut off his head and mangle the body.

The murder happened in June but the remains lay undiscovered until October, when two large leather bags were found in woods to the west of Arreton. The stained and rusty billhook was still recognisable. The dismembered body was not. Only the boy's hat and clothes could be identified. His remains were buried in Arreton Churchyard.

When Morey made no attempt to explain his crime, sentence of death was passed and he was hanged within the hour. His corpse was returned to the Island where it was left rotting on the Downend gibbet until it became 'an offence to eye and nostril'.

The remains were buried in an unmarked grave near the crossroads, and if ever a ghost walked, his should. And of course it does. You may meet it, deadly axe on shoulder, in Burnt House Lane or on Gallows Hill. At the Hare and Hounds inn, the crossbeam of the old gibbet with a notch cut in it beside the date of his execution can still be seen. A ragged figure in leather leggings and jerkin with a floppy black hat with a feather tucked in it has been seen walking there, carrying a big

The lonely Hare and Hounds public house at the top of Gallows Hill where the ghost of Michael Morey is still said to walk, is pictured here in the 1930s

axe with a piece of cloth tied round the blade. Another witness saw him in a greyish-coloured smock with a wide belt round the middle. His arms were twisted behind him, his head lolled on one side. There were holes where eyes should have been, great dark sockets, and shreds of something hanging down his mouth and cheeks.

When James Shutler of Westminster Lane, Newport, saw the ghost, he was driving with his wife Karen and two friends in Burnt House Lane, late one night in 1984. "I can remember it as if it was yesterday. I had to swerve to miss him but when I checked the rear view mirror, nobody was there," he said.

"We were returning from a night out in Newport and had just passed Great Standen when we saw a man walking towards us. My car was a Citroen 2CV so we weren't going fast! We all saw him in the road - I had to brake and swerve for him. We wondered 'what is a bloke carrying an axe doing walking down the road at this time of night'?

"He wore a dark waistcoat, dark trousers or breeches, a stained and dirty shirt with no collar and leather boots. He carried the long-handled axe over his shoulder.

"He radiated a 'horrible feeling' as we passed him; in fact we just wanted to get out of there. It has stuck in my mind all this time, and to this day my wife and I still wonder if it was the ghost of Michael Morey that we saw that night."

PHANTOM CARRIAGE AND FOUR

Leading from the Hare and Hounds at Downend, towards Newport, is Long Lane. It is here that Margaret Speller met a large horse-drawn carriage in the middle of the road, as she drove to work one evening in the early 1990s.

It was still daylight as she turned into Long Lane on the way to Newport. Turning a corner, Margaret saw a fine carriage pulled by four horses, coming towards her. "I slowed right down because the carriage was almost blocking the lane. Although it is two-way, the coach somehow seemed 'too big' for the lane which has high hedges on both sides. I didn't see a coachman, but the carriage, which had a high domed roof, looked ancient."

The horses in their leather harnesses were sweaty and actually steaming after the long climb from Newport. "I remember thinking 'I've got a problem here. How do I get past this?' Then suddenly I was driving right through the carriage! Amazingly, I felt nothing. One moment the carriage was there, the next it had vanished and the road was empty again. I didn't stop. I wasn't frightened, but the whole thing was so very, very strange that I didn't tell anyone. For almost 15 years I put it to the back of my mind, but whenever I drive along that road I can't help remembering what happened there."

GHOST ON A MOTORCYCLE

It was a dark, moonless and foul December night in 1999. The rain was lashing down as business partners John Shimmins and Rosemarie Foster drove back to their hotel in Royal Crescent, Sandown. They had been late-night Christmas shopping in Newport with Rosemarie's daughter, Sarah.

The road through Arreton was deserted, but as they drove towards Apse Heath, in the darkness ahead a solitary motorcyclist appeared suddenly, coming towards them in the middle of the road.

The motorcycle was painted beige or khaki, and it looked like it belonged in a museum. The large central headlamp was unlit, and as the machine came closer on the empty road, the family saw that the rider wore a khaki cape. On his head was an ancient, soft leather helmet. He was looking straight ahead through huge black old-fashioned goggles and didn't move his head at all.

John added, "My van window was open but the old machine made no sound and it is hard to describe, but it was almost as if time slowed down and stopped. I was doing about 30mph as I approached the motorcyclist, but as he appeared, time seemed to stretch. It was as though we were travelling so slowly that we had both stopped; it felt like time itself had stopped. The motorcyclist had a misty appearance. I seemed to be staring at him for ages, then as I became aware of the present moment again, he rode past us and vanished. It was the strangest thing that has ever happened to me.

"Rosemarie and the children asked, 'did you see that?' Young Sarah added, 'that was very strange Mummy'. The whole thing was quite inexplicable, yet it has lingered in my mind very clearly. To this day I can't drive along that stretch of road without thinking of the ghostly motorcyclist," John said.

Rosemarie added, "Something very strange happened that night. Even the way the road was deserted was unusual. As he drew level, it was like we had all the time in the world to look at him – which wasn't possible! I have looked at other motorcyclists since, and have never been able to see them in such detail, especially in the dark. Years later I can still 'see' him vividly and I shiver when I think of that black blankness behind his goggles."

Chapter Eleven

BRIGHSTONE'S MANY GHOSTS

THE PHANTOM HAY WAIN

It was 2.30pm and electrical contractor Mike Toogood and his wife Valerie were driving home towards Brighstone along the 'back' road between Chale and Shorwell, for a late lunch. There was no other traffic around on that summer's afternoon in 2005. Shortly after passing Kingston Church and the ancient manor house, his old Luton van rounded a left-hand bend. Suddenly to his horror, Mike saw a horse-drawn cart coming towards him in the road ahead. He slammed on the brakes. Luckily, he was only doing 28-30mph when the cart appeared in front of him, a few yards ahead.

By the time the van had shuddered to a stop, the cart had vanished into thin air. As Valerie looked up in alarm to see why he had braked, the road was empty again.

"Where on earth did that go?" asked Mike in disbelief. "Where has what gone?" replied Valerie, who had not been looking at the road, so hadn't seen the old cart.

Bewildered and shocked, Mike sat in the van trying to make sense of what he had just seen. "I admit I was stunned. I have worked on farms since I was five years old, so I know a bit about old carts. This one was being pulled by what looked like a brown and white Clydesdale cart-horse. He wasn't well groomed and the old boy was plodding along, blinkered, his head down. There was a chap riding up on the cart, but I didn't register anything about him.

"Everything about the scene seemed to be much too bright - unnaturally bright. It was surreal. The day was sunny, but the light surrounding the hay cart was 'wrong'; there the sun was positively blazing down. The van window had been open but I had heard no sound from the horse and cart.

"Incredibly the road beneath the cart was unpaved; a dusty cart track with stones and bumps. There was a load of hay stacked high on the wain. The cart was about 12 feet long, and the horse was harnessed to a pair of wooden poles or shafts. He was plodding along in the middle of the road as though he was pulling his load uphill, and I had to swerve hard over towards the left hand bank when I saw him. Before the apparition vanished, I had the impression that it was approaching the entrance to a field and was about to turn into it. The whole thing was so weird; it gave me quite a turn. I know I wasn't imagining things but I wish Valerie had seen it too!"

In fact Valerie was not inclined to scoff at Mike's ghost cart, for one night in 2001, she too, had a strange encounter with a ghostly footless figure. Driving past the Countryman pub towards Brighstone, her headlights illuminated the figure of an old man walking his collie dog at the side of the road.

"I pulled out to go around him, but as I glanced at him again, he wasn't there! Then it registered with me that the figure was a ghost – he had been moving along the road but he had no feet."

The couple now live in Moor Lane, Brighstone, but when they occupied an old cottage at Walpen, near Chale, neither Valerie nor the children liked to go upstairs. Then one February night, Mike discovered why. "I couldn't sleep. There was a bright moon shining through the window. Suddenly I was aware that there was the figure of a young woman wearing an old sackcloth dress in the room with me. She appeared solid and was running her fingers through her hair, which was long and tangled.

"I sat up in bed and spoke to her but got no reply. She just vanished. The next night she came again at the same time. I spoke to her again and this time she seemed to be aware of me, although she did not reply. She stood there, seemingly rooted to the spot and running her fingers through her hair once more. I got out of bed and took a couple of steps towards where she was standing, some four or five feet away. Suddenly I noticed she had no feet. Her image ended about four inches above where her ankles should have been. As I moved, she just faded away."

OLD BRIGHSTONE CHURCH

The picturesque village of Brighstone - or Brixton as it was once known - is dominated by the weathered stone church of St Mary the Virgin, dating back over 800 years. The village marked the consecration of three of its rectors as bishops by renaming the local pub, formerly the New Inn, as the Three Bishops.

This religious fervour is odd, because for centuries, smuggling was a major industry and the lonely beaches on the 'Back of the Wight' saw countless clandestine landings of illicit wine, spirits, baccy and lace. Even the old Rectory behind the church boasted a tiny room under the front stairs, said to be a smugglers' hideout. On moonless nights when contraband was due, canny smugglers kept credulous villagers indoors with tales of ghosts and apparitions such as the 'ghastly flying hare' of Moortown Lane!

This misty figure was caught on camera in St Mary's churchyard, Brighstone, in autumn 2005

Graveyard ghost

Rita Godfrey of Chilton Lane, Brighstone, took this intriguing 35mm photograph in St Mary's churchyard at sunset one evening in early September 2005. Returning from taking her dogs for a run on the beach, Rita was struck by a reflection cast by the setting sun, which made the trees appear to be on fire. What she had not noticed was a tall misty shape in the foreground of the picture, just to the right of the old stone church window.

The outline of lichen encrusted tombstones can clearly be seen through the figure, which also appears to have a cowl or hood on its head, while two feet can also be glimpsed on the grass beneath. The gravestones, which date from the early 1800s, are so badly weathered that their inscriptions can no longer be read, so there's no clue to the ghost's identity.

Traditionally every churchyard is said to be haunted by only one ghost - The Watcher - who appears in a long white shroud or winding cloth. This ghost watches over the graves, guarding the dead and waiting for the moment to call on the next person in the parish whose death is ordained....

This picture of the churchyard ghost has been enlarged and the church wall and lichen encrusted gravestones can be seen <u>through</u> the figure

A hooded figure

Rita's husband, Bill Godfrey, also had a strange little story to tell; which may even be connected with Valerie Toogood's experience.

Just before 1am, one summer's night a few years ago, Bill and his dog Buddy were walking home along Limerstone Road after having a jar with friends at the Countryman pub. "I'd had a drink but I was certainly not drunk. There was no traffic about; the road was silent and empty. Suddenly, Buddy started to bark and pull at his lead. Standing motionless at a bus stop was the dark silhouette of a man, his face barely visible under a hood. I couldn't make out his features and although it was a warm night, there was a sense of chill, a feeling of discomfort. With Buddy still barking, I hurried away from that hooded figure, which had moved not at all."

THE COUNTRYMAN GHOST

Across the road at the popular Countryman roadhouse, a spirit known affectionately by staff as 'Fred' lingers in a corner of the function room. He isn't seen – but makes his presence felt nevertheless.

Ann Faulds, who has worked there since the year 2000, explained, "In the far corner of the room where there was once a staircase, you get a strong sensation of being watched by an unseen presence. That area is always colder than the rest of the room and although you don't actually see the ghost, you sometimes get the impression of a shadow flitting past. Early mornings and late at night the feeling is much stronger. I avoid going in there to switch out the lights if I possibly can."

Other staff have also noticed this phenomenon, and have taken to leaving coins on scraps of paper with circles drawn around them in the function room to see if the ghost moves them!

The pub spirit is known as 'Fred' after the former owner Fred

Handley, who bought the property in the 1950s and opened it as The Casa Espanol. It was originally built in 1938 as a garage, but when the war intervened the empty building became a potato store and was later used for manufacturing concrete blocks.

After obtaining an alcohol, music and late-night licence, Fred Handley horrified local clergy when he built a glass dance floor there (most ladies wore skirts in those days) amid fears that people might watch proceedings from beneath. The floor was built however, and the Casa Espanol - named in honour of Fred and his wife Edith's many visits to Spain, became very popular.

Following Fred's death there in 1975, the Casa as it was known locally, continued under various owners until it was renamed The Countryman in 1989.

In 2007, the local branch of the Campaign for Real Ale described it as: *"A friendly country roadhouse with an enthusiastic landlord. This fine family pub enjoys a reputation for good food, fine beer and is a regular finalist in the local CAMRA Pub of the Year competition. The large function room is popular for wedding receptions and evening gatherings."*

Perhaps they should add that it is haunted too … as all good pubs should be!

SPIRITS AT THE THREE BISHOPS

Brighstone once boasted two inns, The Five Bells and The New Inn, which stood next to one another. Today the old thatched Five Bells is the newsagent and Brighstone Store. The New Inn, a former coaching inn with 'stables, guestrooms and pleasure garden' was extensively renovated in the 1920s, and renamed the Three Bishops in 1977.

Two ghosts have been seen here. One is a young girl, aged seven or eight. The other is an older woman, who regulars and landlords affectionately call Maggie, after a former landlady. The pub also has cold spots, which are evident when Maggie is around.

Kath Wright encountered the young spirit a number of times when she and her partner Billy stayed in the flat above the bar in May 2006. Both described a young girl with dark, wavy hair and a deathly pale face. Billy had a close encounter with her on his way to the bathroom in the middle of the night. Still half asleep, he almost bumped into the ghost in a room above the oldest part of the pub. She wore dark clothes and as Billy brushed past, he actually felt her hair. Without thinking he said, "Excuse me" and stepped around her. Then realisation struck and he looked back to see what he had touched. The girl had vanished.

The pub changed hands in September 2006, when new licensees Chris and Helen Hessey, their three children and Jess the cat moved in. Helen has had several encounters with Maggie. This ghost, which is dressed in yellow or orange and has long brown hair, is seen crossing the dining room, and where she walks, the room is always cold.

Screwdrivers hold a special fascination for Maggie. Several have vanished from the flat upstairs only to reappear downstairs, where they are usually found behind the bar.

At night when all the lights go off, the footsteps start. The 'tap tap' of light footsteps in the corridor outside the bedrooms is heard, usually fifteen minutes after the family has gone to bed. At other times, a dragging sound is heard, and furniture is moved.

Taps are another favourite. Chris often finds the hot tap running in the kitchen, when he is positive that he has turned it off. This has been happening for years, and previous landlords have found taps turned on all over the pub.

Brighstone in the early 1900s showing the New Inn, which is now the Three Bishops

One morning when Helen and one of the cleaners were enjoying an early coffee in the bar, they both heard a loud bang behind them. They were suddenly overcome by a sensation of light-headedness and felt violently sick.

Similar manifestations

Over the years, other landlords have reported similar manifestations at the pub. When John Knowles was licensee from 1985 to 1990, he was often aware of Maggie. There were footsteps, scraping noises, doors would open and taps would be turned on, including beer taps behind the bar. "I lost a lot of beer through that," he complained.

One night John was woken by a noise. He switched on the light in time to see a wing of the three-sided mirror on the dressing table turn to face him. He pushed it back in place and put a vase in front to wedge it in place. When he was back in bed, the mirror moved again. "Finally I said out loud, 'Maggie, for heaven's sake leave it alone and let me get some sleep'."

When John moved to a bedroom above the kitchen, he was alone one night when the door opened. "I shot out of bed to see who was there. The corridor was empty so I put the Yale deadlock on. Within minutes, the door opened again. I knew it was Maggie, so I told her that it was late, I wanted my sleep, and for her to go and get some rest.

"My mother was a medium, so I'm not afraid of spirits. I believe that there was a landlady here called Maggie many years ago, so perhaps she is still around keeping an eye on 'her pub'. I think she is a harmless dear who likes to know what's going on and is just letting you know she is around."

Two nights running in 2007, the pub's CCTV captured ghostly goings-on at the front door. Landlord Chris said, "On 23rd March at 11.31pm, the pub was shut and we were clearing up when the door opened on its own, then a few seconds later it closed again.

"We looked outside but the road was empty. When we checked the CCTV film, the glass-panelled door could be seen opening and closing on its own.

"The following night at 11.25pm just as we were telling two friends, it happened again. The door opened and closed again in a very deliberate way. We were speechless.

"Again we checked the security tape; again there was no one there. But we could see the outline of a disembodied arm through the glass…"

GHOST OF WAYTES COURT

The 16th century farmhouse of Wayte's Court, Brighstone, once housed the manorial court. Since the 1960s, it has been occupied by the Wannop family, who run a timber and fencing business at the 400-acre farm.

Julie Wannop was aged thirteen in 1985, when she saw a man's ghost in the old farm stables one winter's afternoon. Recalling that encounter, she said, "I was bedding the horses down for the night at around 4.30pm. I was working with my back to the door when 'something' made me turn round. Standing about six feet away from me was the outline of a bearded man in a long coat and knee-length boots. His head was bare but he carried a hat in his hand.

"He didn't look at me, but gazed at the horses for almost a minute before walking forwards and vanishing. I didn't dare to move although I wasn't really scared. I just stood watching him; I didn't know what to do. I knew he was a ghost. As soon as I had finished with the horses, I went indoors where Mum took one look at me and asked, 'What on earth's the matter? You look like you have seen a ghost'."

Curiously, the horses appeared unconcerned by the apparition, although Julie and her mum, Lynda, noticed that occasionally they would refuse to enter the stables and seemed 'spooked' by something unseen there.

Chapter Twelve

GHOSTS AT SCHOOL

THE PHANTOM KING

As one of Newport's oldest and most historic buildings, it is only right that the King James I Grammar School, which since 1618 has stood at the corner of Lower St James' Street and Lugley Street, should be haunted.

King Charles I stayed there for sixty days in September 1648 while negotiating the Treaty of Newport. He used the oak-panelled schoolroom as his presence chamber and slept in the room above. It was there, at dawn on November 30, that the king was seized by the Army and taken to London for his trial and execution.

The building's role as a school ended in 1963, and five years later it became a youth centre owned by the local authority. Supernatural activity is centred around the headmaster's office and the room above, in which the king slept.

Footsteps are heard echoing through deserted rooms when the building is empty. One youth leader who spent a night in that bedroom, wouldn't go back again. Although it was the middle of summer, the room went icy cold, he said.

In 2006, Chris Smy, who works in the old headmaster's office, was with colleague Jan Meechan collating papers on a table in the middle of the historic oak-panelled room. He said, "The telephone directory suddenly jumped off the old carved oak overmantel, flew across the room and landed on

A ghostly hand sweeps books off this shelf

The former King James I Grammar School, where King Charles I stayed in 1648

the table, spilling Jan's coffee. Objects left on that mantelpiece overnight often 'fall' off despite there being a deep lip. Staff find papers swept off it and scattered on the floor, as though by an impatient hand.

One day, Ivor King had a meeting with a junior club leader in that room. This lady who was psychic, sat facing the door. "As we were talking, she stared past me towards the door. She said, 'It's the headmaster, he's just popped in.' Then she explained that she had just seen the ghost of a man in an old-fashioned black mortar-board cap and long gown, step into the room, then vanish."

In the former stables, now the main youth centre, where school horses were once stabled, the old sweet aroma of hay and straw occasionally fills the air and sometimes the heavy tread of riding boots is heard mounting the stairs. Youth leaders have also reported hearing balls being knocked around on the pool table when they are locking up and alone, late at night.

Haunted youth centres
Other youth centres have their own ghost stories. At Wootton in the former village school premises in New Road, leader in charge, Rachael Knight, has heard the sound of an old piano playing in the empty building. "I have heard it on several occasions, usually late in the afternoon, when I am alone there. The caretaker has also reported a ghostly presence in the old school, and often feels he is being watched."

At Ryde Youth Centre, a warm, friendly presence has been felt by staff when they are locking up the premises - a former church - at night.

Meanwhile at the former town hall in Grafton Street, now Sandown Youth Centre, Chris Smy saw a small ghostly shape appear through the panels of a glass door, then it 'whizzed' away at high speed. This phenomenon was accompanied by a very sharp fall in temperature, which was noticed by other colleagues.

OLD WEST STREET SCHOOL

Generations of Newport children passed through the gates of West Street Primary School to learn the 'three Rs'. The old, red brick Church of England 'National School' was originally built in 1816 on the edge of the town's cricket ground. When it was rebuilt in 1909 at a cost of £5,000, it could take over 700 infants and children.

All that now remains of the school and its playgrounds after demolition in the 1990s are two horse chestnut trees, which once provided shade - and plenty of conkers - for its pupils. Today, Chestnut Court, a large block of flats built by South Wight Housing Association, occupies the site.

Named after the row of trees that once lined the school wall, it was opened in 1996 by Southampton Football Club's former manager, Lawrie McMenemy. So when Trish Cullen and her children, Christopher and Sam, moved into their apartment overlooking Carisbrooke Road in 1999, she never dreamed it would be haunted.

Trish explained, "Soon after we moved in, a tiny cactus plant on Chris's bedroom window-sill disappeared. The pot was still there, but the plant vanished. Then one night I was watching television when the

Old West Street primary school was built in 1816 and rebuilt in 1909. It was demolished in the 1990s

channel changed on its own; it still does this at times; moving up and down the channels. When I got up to switch it back, I saw that the cactus had reappeared on the window-sill. It seems to me that everything which happens in the flat is just mischievous and childish; as though whatever is here just wants us to know it's around. The next thing to vanish was my daughter's favourite pair of 'Dulux' dog novelty slippers. She left them beside the bed and when she woke, they were missing. A few days later, they turned up again, inside her duvet on her bed.

"One night when I was in bed, I heard an almighty noise that I can only describe as sounding like a wheelbarrow full of rubble being tipped out in the hall. Since then both children have heard it and I still hear it occasionally, during the day and sometimes at night. We have also seen an ashtray move by itself across the lounge table, and watched as one of my birthday cards moved from one side of the television to the other.

"We hear someone pacing up and down in our hallway - by day and by night. I hear the floor creaking as 'someone' walks around in the hall with slow but light steps."

At 3am one night, the ghost showed itself at last. When Sam's friend Laura stayed overnight, she woke to go to the bathroom. As she passed Chris's room, Laura was astonished to see a young boy, perhaps eight or nine years old, standing by the bed, staring sadly at the sleeping boy.

The ghostly child wore a piece of dirty cloth wrapped around his bare feet. He had dark blonde hair, and Laura noticed he was wearing tattered trousers which went to just below his knee. The boy also wore a shirt covered with bloodstains and mud, and a cap, which in the light from the street lamp outside was a greyish colour. One of his eyes appeared red and very bloodshot. "I think he saw me because he jumped a little. I just stared at him for a minute or so, then I ran to wake Sam up to go to the bathroom with me," said Laura.

Trish added, "When my mother and brother died, I sensed the spirit boy was often around me. My neighbour Tanya, who can see him, said he would just stand at my side staring up at me. At other times, she sees him gazing fixedly at the television. Although weeks go by when I don't sense him, I always know when he is around for I feel a cold sensation moving about the living room and my legs get chilly when he stands near me. It doesn't bother me, but I do feel that he is a sad little soul and it would be better if he moved on to find peace."

Whispering her name...

Theirs is not the only flat where ghosts are seen. Nearby, a woman in Victorian dress has been glimpsed walking up the hallway and disappearing through a wall. Julie Wolf, who formerly lived next door to

Pupils at West Street School are pictured in the playground

Trish, would hear an unseen presence whispering her name, 'Julie, Julie' but never saw who called her. Another tenant hears the sound of cups and glasses being rattled in the empty kitchen at odd times. When her son was younger, he would talk to, and play happily with another unseen child in the flat - which she found very unsettling.

Tanya Shepherd, who moved to Chestnut Court in 2002, has heard the ghost of a young girl giggling in her flat a few doors away from Trish. "I have never seen her but she is quite mischievous and she likes to move or borrow small things, such as keys, coins and pieces of jewellery. She doesn't keep them long, only a couple of hours as a rule, but she puts them back somewhere different, and that's usually when I hear that little giggle. One day, she took my keys and I found them later in the deep-freeze!"

Tanya, who has 'seen' ghosts since she was a child, frequently catches sight of the young, pale-faced ghost-boy in Trish's flat.

Aged about eight and looking very solemn, Tanya sees him wearing a dirty white shirt and long trousers with baggy bottoms. Unlike in Laura's description, Tanya sees shoes with buckles on the ghostly child's feet.

"I don't see him as a solid figure, he's more of an outline with some colour, rather like a reflection. As soon as he is about, I go cold. He doesn't do much; he likes to stand in the living room, often for a couple of hours at a time, and seems fascinated by the television. He stands and just stares at it. Otherwise, if there are other children around, he watches them instead. I sense that he had an accident at school and died in the playground. One day, when I was talking to Trish and he was in the room, we said we wanted to know how he had died. At that moment, he came over to me and poked me on the arm," said Tanya.

She added, "In 2006 when Trish got out her Christmas decorations, the ghost-boy was entranced and seemed particularly taken with an illuminated Santa Claus. He stood by it for several hours just gazing at Father Christmas' figure. I don't think he had enjoyed much Christmas spirit in his short life."

Named after the row of 'conker' trees that once lined the school wall, Chestnut Court was built in 1996 on the site of old West Street Primary School

GOODNIGHT DORIS!

Nearby in Carisbrooke Road is a former alehouse which was the family home of Newport garage proprietor Barry Price for many years. It subsequently became a Bed and Breakfast establishment run by Barry's wife, Trina.

During this time, the ghostly activity revolved around the front room downstairs. Trina was aware of a woman's presence there. "I knew it was a lady and she stood at the window, watching. I felt her name was Doris. She was often around and she moved things. I was upset when we sold the place, and I think the ghost picked up on my distress.

"A clairvoyant friend who came to look around picked up the name Dolly or Dottie and the spirit of a child called William. She thought 'something' had happened to him and that he had died young."

The cottage was at one time used as an alehouse. Long ago, a local gentleman is thought to have established his pregnant lover there, and Trina suspects that this lady is the one haunting her old house.

One day Trina was standing in the living room when her foot sank *into* the floor. "My heart started racing and I burst into tears. I was pushed backwards and forwards, then it calmed down and my foot was free again.

"On another occasion, I was with several friends in that room. Curiously, in the centre it was very hot, while near the window, where the figure stands, it felt freezing cold."

Another friend told Trina she had felt rooted to the ground in that room, and for a few seconds had been unable to move or speak.

"On 30th September 2005, as the Bed and Breakfast business closed down, I started to feel uneasy. I thought I could smell smoke there and sometimes when we spoke about the house, fire alarms would go off. Finally, I got so fed up with this that I removed the batteries. Then I asked, 'Doris, are you looking for William?' There was no reply.

"Although I was alone in the house, I would always say 'Goodnight Doris. Look after the house', as I left. That night as I locked the front door and turned to leave, I looked back.

"There was a small face at the front room window peering out at me. It was definitely a woman, and there seemed to be a blue light around her. I know it was Doris, and she was watching me leave."

SKELETONS AND SKULLS

Archaeologists are used to handling the remains and artefacts of the dead. Excavating, conserving and cataloguing finds is what they do. But here on the Island, the archaeologists' work is overseen by a ghost.

The Island's Archaeology and Historic Environment Service occupies an old Infant school in Clatterford Road, Carisbrooke. Built in 1836 for 80 children, and enlarged in 1878, the school also had teachers' living accommodation above. Here, in the Victorian schoolhouse, among boxes of artefacts and treasures, bones and skulls, the ghost, thought to

A former teacher haunts this old school

be a woman, is heard but seldom seen. Occasionally, Archaeologist and Finds Liaison Officer Frank Basford, hears light footsteps on the stairs when he is working alone at night. "I have also heard the sound of the front door opening and people coming in, but when I check, there's nobody there. Sometimes I see 'something' flit past in the shadows. A security guard, who has since left, saw a ghostly figure in the locked building one night. Occasionally the alarm system goes off too. At first we blamed the bats, but perhaps a former schoolmistress is still around and keeping an eye on things."

This was confirmed by medium Leslie George when he visited the old school early one evening in July 2007. The kindly spirit of a woman in her fifties appeared, standing outside the front of the building, smiling gently. When he asked her name, Les was told that she was known as 'Miss'. But of course, if she was a teacher there, that's what the children would have called her.

Chapter Thirteen

A MISCELLANY OF GHOSTS

On the outskirts of Newport lies Shide, an ancient settlement which is recorded in the Domesday Book. Centuries ago, Shide Bridge was the meeting place for the organisation of the Island's defences. On nearby St George's Down in 1625, Island Governor, the Earl of Southampton, built a fine bowling green and pavilion for local gentry. Here, up to 40 'Knights and Gentlemen' gathered to play bowls and cards on Tuesdays and Thursdays. Today, Shide has been almost absorbed by Newport, but linger there and you may meet some of its ghostly characters ...

EMPTY CHAIR AT THE BARLEY MOW

If you see an empty chair by the fireplace at the Barley Mow, please don't sit there, for it belongs to Jack, the pub ghost. Locals politely avoid the seat, but unwary visitors may find they are sharing the chair with the resident spirit.

Since Sue and Reg Phillips became licensees in 1997, 'old Jack' has made himself at home there and attached himself to Sue. Jack, who was probably once a regular at the pub, is an elderly ghost in his late sixties with greying hair, wearing a white shirt with a high-necked collar.

Sporting a thick tweed waistcoat over his pot belly, tweed trousers and brown boots, he sits contentedly in the corner, smoking his pipe - although since July 2007 this has been an offence punishable by a fine!

Jack can be mischievous, and welcomes new landlords by sending a bottle of whisky flying across the room. "He seems happy here and we are happy to have him," smiled Sue. "We often smell his pipe tobacco, especially late in the evening. I always wish him good morning or good night and I think he appreciates this. He is a sweet old man."

Sue believes Jack may have worked at the railway station, which was next door to the pub, or even at nearby St George's chalk pit. Shide station was a part of the Isle of Wight Central Railway, and in 1895 a spur was laid at Shide through a short tunnel into the pit itself so that chalk could be transported to lime kilns and cement mills.

Late one very wet night, Sue glanced out of the front window to see a woman dressed in army uniform dating from the World War Two era,

The Barley Mow at Shide. This photo was taken before the original pub was extensively altered in the 1930s

walking along the footpath towards the pub. As Sue watched, the figure reached the lamppost opposite… and vanished.

PETS AT REST

Sue Hemmings owns the tranquil Pets At Rest pet cemetery, set on a quiet hillside acre just outside Newport. Located at Pan Cottages, near Shide Chalk Pit, the cemetery opened in 1985. Sue moved there in 1998.

Over the years, many beloved pets have been laid to rest there. Occasionally Sue sees their spirits around the place. "Usually I glimpse them out of the corner of my eye but it certainly doesn't worry me," she said.

One ghostly animal actually visited the cemetery in the back of a car. "A couple arrived to collect the ashes of their dog and to bury them here. They were accompanied by a German shepherd dog, which sat looking nervous and very uncomfortable on the back seat of the car.

"Next to him was a big, handsome boxer dog, sitting there proudly and very upright. He was a strong, muscular intelligent-looking dog. I smiled at the boxer; he grinned back at me. We actually made eye contact," Sue said.

"I fetched the ashes and asked the owners if they wanted to bring the dogs to the burial. They looked puzzled, so I said it was OK for the boxer and shepherd to come along.

"They looked at me again. 'We have never had a boxer. There's only our German shepherd in the car,' they told me. They had only bought the car a couple of weeks earlier, so who that beautiful ghost dog was, remains a mystery. It does explain why the German shepherd looked so uncomfortable though," laughed Sue.

The old cottage at Pan, built on Church land in the 1600s, was once a single, large thatched dwelling. Now divided in two, Sue's cottage is haunted by the ghost of an elderly man who wears a flat cap and gaiters. Her daughter, Vicki, who has seen spirits since she was a small girl, has glimpsed this apparition in her bedroom, as well as other spirits who linger there.

Vicki said, "One sunny day, I was on my own in the cottage. I had just come out of the shower and was walking across the hall to my bedroom, when I saw a little girl. She had long blonde hair in ringlets and wore a long-sleeved Victorian dress with cuffs. She ran in front of me, jumped onto the bed, threw a sheet over her head, then disappeared."

Years later, Vicki had another strange encounter. "When we first moved here I was with my friend, Steve, and we were in the spare room. Steve went to the bathroom and as I sat there in bed, the top half of a man appeared between me and the bathroom door.

"I could only see his shoulders and face. He appeared to be in his late forties and was quite solid. He had slicked-back hair and wore a dark jacket with a cravat at his throat. I out called to Steve, 'There is a man just behind you!' As I spoke, the figure floated gently backwards and vanished into the wall."

Ghost with a walking stick
August 11th 2005 was a warm, sunny day and Vicki went out with her friend Marie, to pick sloes and blackberries from the hedgerows in Pan Lane and St George's Way.

Vicki recalled, "I was stooping to put a handful of berries into my bucket when, out of the corner of my eye, I saw a little old lady with a walking stick crossing the main road. I remember thinking, 'I hope she gets across OK' and as I turned to watch, she disappeared. I told Marie, 'I think I have just seen a ghost!'

"When I said it was an old lady, Marie asked me what she looked like. I said she had grey hair, and although it was a hot day, she was wearing a long, tan mackintosh, and held a wooden walking stick in her left hand. 'I know her!' Marie exclaimed. 'She always used to walk that road with a little dog. It wasn't hers; she walked it for someone. But she's been dead for years'."

When Vicki told her mum what had happened, Sue also recognised the description. "She was a little frail old woman who lived in a cottage near the chalk pit. She shuffled around in 'sensible' walking shoes and most days she would cross the main road and walk along the riverbank into Newport. How strange that her ghost still walks the same path."

This photograph of Shide in the 1930s was taken from St Georges Down. The Barley Mow and Shide station can be seen to the right of the main road

SHIDE SHADE

Another ghost has been seen by the riverbank at Shide. This one also wore a long coat but was definitely male. Simon, who lives in Pan Lane, was walking home with a friend at 4am, just before dawn one summer morning, in 1995.

As the men strolled along the river towards Newport, they noticed a bearded man in a long leather coat and hat moving in front of them.

"He came out of the darkness and passed between us. He was really close; the footpath, which is on the old railway track is about six feet wide there, and he almost brushed my shoulder as he strode past.

"He made no sound and didn't look at us as he passed by. The whole thing was so strange that my friend and I both turned to watch him. But he wasn't there. He had vanished.

We were both shaken, although we laughed and said 'We've just seen a ghost!' He had looked solid and real, although the way he was dressed reminded me of a Guy Fawkes figure."

ORB AT SHIDE

One late Autumn night in the early 1980s, Nigel Cantelo and two friends were out walking in the woods at St George's Down, above Shide chalk pit, when a mysterious glowing 'orb' light appeared on the path in front of them.

Nigel who lives at Collingwood Road, Newport, explained, "As kids we often played in those woods and the chalk pit, where the cliff face is known as 'Dead Man's Drop' because people have had bad falls there! That night we had our catapults with us and were looking for pigeons and pheasants – we were young then and we didn't know any better!" he added. "It was a clear still night; so quiet you could have heard a pin drop. Walking up a small path through the trees, we spotted a light about 50 yards ahead. The size of a tennis ball, it hung at about chest height and glowed with an intense orange light. We all stopped; the silence was absolute. This light was gliding slowly towards us down the path. We retreated about 100 yards and turned again. The light was still 50 yards away. We walked away again, until we were right on the edge of the cliff. The light was still coming. We looked at one another, and then went over the edge, sliding down the steep chalk face right to the floor of the pit.

"If only we had been brave enough to walk towards it and shine our torches at the orb. But we weren't! Years later, while metal detecting nearby, we found an urn buried there. I know people have their ashes scattered in that area. Could the ghost light be connected with this?"

VITTLEFIELDS GHOST

Author's note: the following story is one of the very rare occasions when I may have seen a ghost myself!

"Did you see that strange lady, Nanny?" asked Tia as we drove along the Forest Road towards Yarmouth, one morning in August 2006.

In fact, I *had* noticed the curiously-dressed young woman who crossed the road in front of us on the double bend at Vittlefields Farm. She caught my attention because of her strange old-fashioned attire, and I, too, had been wondering about her.

It was 9.30am on a bright sunny morning and I was driving my six-year-old granddaughter, Tia, to her swimming lesson at Freshwater. Visibility was excellent and we both had a clear view of the tall young woman, wearing a full-length skirt and long-sleeved jacket in a dusky pink gingham fabric. Her hair was brown and on her head she wore a close-fitting white lace-trimmed cap, tied in a bow under her chin.

Turning into the first bend, we both looked to see where the young woman was going. But there was no one there. She had vanished. "That was a funny lady," commented Tia, as I looked back in my mirror. Before confirming what I had seen, I asked Tia to describe the lady - which she did - right down to the white 'handkerchief' on her head. The description tallied with what I had seen. "Do you think she was a ghost, Nanny?" Tia asked excitedly.

"No. I expect the lady lives nearby and was dressed like that for a special reason," I replied. "But on our way back, we will call in at those buildings to ask the people who work there if they know the lady, or why she was in old-fashioned clothes."

Later that day we stopped at the farm buildings, now converted into several small business units. After describing what we had seen, we were met with blank looks. No, everyone assured us, no young woman in a long skirt had visited that morning, and no one living nearby wore such clothes.

They were intrigued but unable to help. So the mystery remains. Who was the woman? Why she had apparently crossed the road on such a dangerous bend and vanished? Then I remembered …

The ghost's warning

Could this be the same spirit that walks in Betty Haunt Lane nearby? As the name suggests it has a reputation for being haunted. As the mist rolls across the lane, strange things can happen, for here the shade of Betty, the smuggler's daughter who met a bad end two centuries ago, is said to walk.

Betty fell in love with an Excise officer and betrayed her comrades who were hiding their contraband at the nearby Blacksmiths Arms Inn. Most of them were captured, but a few escaped. They came back for

Betty's ghost was seen at the end of Betty Haunt Lane

Betty. Her death was slow and painful, and it is said that her screams and moans may still be heard on misty nights in Betty Haunt Lane.

Where the lane meets Forest Road at Vittlefields Cross is the former site of the Isle of Wight Donkey Sanctuary (now located in Wroxall). It's here in 1988 that Charlie Clarke, who runs the charity with his wife Cherryl, received a warning from a ghost.

Charlie was working at the sanctuary one summer afternoon when his labrador, Ben, started barking furiously. Standing at the gate Charlie saw a woman aged about twenty-five. She wore old-fashioned, shabby clothes and, speaking very slowly in a broad Isle of Wight accent, she told Charlie that she lived in a cottage 'down the lane'.

The strange young woman warned him, "You must never come here without the dog when the mist comes across," she urged - not once but five times. Promising to return, she wished Charlie 'Good-day'.

Charlie said goodbye and turned back to the stables, feeling extremely relieved that she had gone. There was something distinctly strange about her. She was very dull-witted, almost stupid, and he had been uneasy talking to her.

As he walked away from the woman, Charlie noticed his hair was standing on end and he felt icy cold. Turning back towards the gate, he saw she had vanished. He looked up and down the lane for her, even climbing the gate to peer over the hedge, but she was nowhere to be found.

"I had been talking to a ghost and it is something I never want to do again," admitted Charlie. "Despite her promise she never returned." Since his encounter with the ghost, he often felt uneasy, as if he was being watched. And until the sanctuary moved to Wroxall a few years later, if fog rolled across the valley as darkness fell, Charlie heeded her warning. He never visited the donkeys ... unless his dog was with him. Visit the sanctuary at: *www.iwdonkey-sanctuary.com*

CANTEEN ROAD GHOST

Canteen Road is so named because the area was once an encampment for Prussian troops, who were garrisoned there, before they left to fight alongside the British against Napoleon at Waterloo. The same site was later used to house French prisoners of war.

A young woman, unwittingly, picked up a ghostly hitchhiker on her way home from Godshill, one night in the early 1990s. Sharon Fox now living at Sandown, had visited a friend and was driving along Canteen Road when she was suddenly aware of 'someone' in the car with her.

"It was a very powerful feeling, as though somebody had just sat up in the back of the car. I was so shocked that I swerved, because I thought someone had hidden there to attack me. As I looked in my mirror, it dawned on me it wasn't a maniac sitting in the back, but a ghost. What I saw was like an x-ray photograph of a balding middle-aged man. He was quite muscular and wore a white shirt. I didn't sense any menace, just a strong feeling that he was trying to get somewhere.

"I told him, 'I do not want to give you a lift. Go away!' But he didn't go immediately, he stayed in the car until we had passed Princelett Shute. That's where he vanished. The car immediately felt different and I knew I was on my own again.

"I am not easily scared, and have seen ghosts before, but this was the strangest experience I have ever had. A few years later, a motorist died on that same stretch of road and I wondered whether she, too, saw that ghost in her car and swerved, with tragic consequences."

COWES GHOST-SHIP

The year was 1941 and early one Saturday afternoon, young Arthur Lewis was on board a Red Funnel paddle steamer crossing from Cowes to Southampton. It was the middle of the war and although more than 60 years have passed, he still remembers a strange incident that has puzzled him ever since.

Although it was early May, the weather was atrocious; it was blowing a gale and rain was sheeting in almost horizontally. Arthur, an apprentice joiner, had been sent to JS Whites shipyard with other builders to help repair bomb damage caused in the Blitz. Returning home, he was on the leeward side of the ferry, sheltering with two friends.

Now retired and living near Southampton, Arthur recalled, "I must have been about 17-years-old at the time. As the ferry turned across the wind, the paddle-wheel lifted out of the water, and we slowed almost to a standstill.

"Suddenly, a fully-rigged four-masted sailing ship loomed out of the rain from the direction of Gurnard, about three hundred yards from us. The hull was yellow and with all sails billowing, it was pulling hard into the teeth of the gale. I turned to the other chaps and said, 'Hey, look at that!' We could not believe what we were seeing. The vessel was sailing hard in the wrong direction against the wind, which was impossible.

While travelling to Southampton aboard a Red Funnel paddle steamer, Arthur Lewis saw a four-masted ghost ship sailing off Cowes

There was no sound of sails flapping, the old wooden ship made no noise, and as the ferry picked up speed again, the apparition vanished."

COWES PURITANS

Firework Night is the explosive finale to Cowes Week, and the town is at its busiest that day. So when visitors Sheilah Legg and her late husband from Havant, fancied a cup of tea, they feared the cafes would be full.

"It was August 1992, and my husband and I were in Cowes for the fireworks. We found an old bakery and teashop in the High Street. The tables downstairs were full but when we went upstairs, we were surprised to find ourselves alone. As we awaited service, I was struck by a feeling of deep peace and absolute stillness. There was no sound from downstairs. I became aware of figures in the empty room with us. A man and woman in what appeared to be puritan dress were murmuring in low voices. I couldn't make out the words. They were going about their work as they talked. The sun was streaming into the room. Time had ceased to exist.

"This interlude was short-lived as a family arrived in the café and with much noise, they trooped upstairs to join us. The peace was shattered and the images vanished. When I commented on what had happened to my husband, he said he hadn't noticed anything! I shall always wonder about it. I can't remember what the teashop was called but I know it was on the left side of the main street near The Parade."

Roman ghosts

Sheilah continued, "In April 2006, my partner and I decided to visit the Roman Villa at Brading. I had been a couple of times before. As we walked round and I got to the area where the doorway was (now covered by stonework from the portico), I again had that feeling of deep quiet and peace.

"Suddenly I was 'seeing' a line of several Roman sandalled feet walking away to my left as I faced the original entrance. There were four lines marching in pairs. I could see their feet in laced leather sandals, their ankles and lower legs. It was a surprise to see them coming from under the apse (a semicircular projection) until I realised, that would have been the original level of the doorway into the corridor. Again,

The visitors' centre at Brading Roman Villa, where Roman ghosts are seen

children arrived and their noise broke the spell. I could hardly believe what I had seen and wondered if I had imagined it; yet, I knew I had not.

"I went to the reception desk and asked staff if they had ever seen ghosts. They hadn't, but they told me that a visiting medium had seen those same Roman sandalled feet walking down the corridor to the healing room,

"Well," I said, "I have just seen the same thing, and I'm not a medium. Since I was a girl, I have had a sense of being 'told things' but apart from glimpsing family members after they died, I never saw ghosts until I went to the Isle of Wight!"

APSE HEATH MYSTERY

Not far from the Fighting Cocks public house at Apse Heath stands a house, which proved to be anything but ordinary when Christine Jennings and her family moved there in 1993.

She explained, "The property was almost new, so there was no reason to suspect it was haunted. I first noticed something was not right when I felt constantly uneasy in the hall; I just hated being there.

"When I vacuumed, the Hoover would often switch itself off. I listened to tapes while cleaning and these too, would switch themselves off. Then things started to get worse.

"We ran a shoe shop in Sandown, and on my day off, I enjoyed a 'lie-in'. The first time ghosts appeared I thought I was dreaming (although I knew I wasn't). As I lay dozing, I heard the bedroom door open.

"Then two young children ran around the bed, laughing and playing. I wanted to open my eyes and tell them off - because I thought that it was my daughters - but I couldn't move. Then I became aware of someone standing by the bed. I was terrified. My right side felt as if a current of electricity was passing through it. It was as if something was trying to get inside me. This person started to tap on my head. Still I didn't dare move.

"Then I was aware of an antiquated telephone on a little table moving towards the bed (we didn't have a telephone or a table there). It started to ring with an old-fashioned ring. When everything went quiet, I plucked up courage to move. I ran into the front room expecting my husband and daughters to be there. The house was empty. Later, when I told my husband what had happened, he laughed and said I had been dreaming. I convinced myself that he was right. But it kept happening…

"It was always the same sequence of events and only happened when I was there on my own. I persuaded my husband we should move into the back bedroom, and put my daughters in the front room instead.

"However after just one night, my eldest daughter refused to sleep there because she had been woken by the bedroom door opening and had seen a man standing beside her bed. We didn't escape the ghost in the back bedroom either. I would wake in the night to hear someone walking about in the attic above. My husband said it was just birds.

"Eventually he went up into the attic with a neighbour, but found nothing there. My husband continued ridiculing me until one night when he woke me in the early hours in a state of terror. He had heard those footsteps at last!

"By now I was at my wits' end. I told a friend in Freshwater who offered to 'cleanse' the house with her healing group.

"A few days later we had people to stay, so my husband went to buy some beer. I was hanging a coat up in the entrance hall when I saw a pair of feet standing by the toilet door. Thinking he had returned, I said to my husband, 'You weren't long!' Then I realised that the legs ended at the knees. There was no body.

"Later that night, I had a strange dream about a shabby old farm worker who was trying to get through the garden gate. Then there was a loud bang and I woke, knowing that the man in my dream was the one haunting us. When I rang my healer friend in Totland to tell her what had happened, she said that was the night when she and her group had cleansed the house with prayers.

"I don't think the ghost was trying to cause us any harm. He was trying to get in touch the only way he knew how. But I don't understand why it happened in such a new house. I think that old-fashioned telephone was like a symbol meaning, 'we want to talk to you'. I only ever heard the ghost children; a boy and girl aged six or seven, when I was on my own. That house was a strange place and I was not sorry to leave."

GHOST AT PRAYER

The devout ghost of an elderly woman was a regular visitor to an old property at Ryde until her little shrine was dismantled during renovation works.

It was always at night when Mike Rashley, who lived at the converted coach house, saw the elderly woman kneeling at prayer. The house and stables near Ryde Cemetery were built in 1850 and Mike's bedroom was once a small chapel. After moving in, he saw the old lady at her devotions three times in four months. She would always appear between 10pm and 11pm.

Mike added, "She remained visible for between 15 to 30 seconds each time. She wore an old-fashioned black dress, a black lace shawl covering her grey hair, which was in a bun. There was some light in the corner of the room where I would see her profile as she knelt silently at her prayers. When she vanished, it was as though someone had switched off a light. She was there one moment, gone the next. I wasn't afraid, for there was a tranquil atmosphere surrounding her. I don't think she was aware of me - or the modern surroundings of my bedroom."

Mike believed he knew who the religious ghost was. For when he bought his home in the early 1960s, the coach house was part of a larger estate belonging to an elderly lady and her two sons, one of whom was a missionary. The lady, a devout Roman Catholic, had set up her own shrine in the tack room of the coach house, complete with incense burners and a kneeler.

"I never actually met her, for she died in 1962 as I was buying the place," said Mike. "I actually had to dismantle this little chapel when I converted the coach house into living accommodation. There was a doorway, which the old lady used when she came from the big house to use her shrine. This has since been bricked over. After I removed the altar and renovated the room, the old lady's visits stopped abruptly. I have always been quite sceptical about ghosts and the supernatural but I can't explain this any other way."

Sadly, Mike has died since telling me about this elderly ghost. His wife Margaret, who lived at the old coach house with him from 1994 until 2005, has kindly allowed me to tell Mike's story.

'I DREADED THE NIGHTS...'

Fiona Renshaw spent ten years at her ground floor flat in Augusta Road, Ryde. Now living in Ireland, she remembers the feelings of dread she experienced at night there.

"It was during the winter of 1990, two years after my partner and I moved there, that I saw the ghost. I was alone in the flat as my partner was working a night shift. I went to bed at 11.30pm and was trying to get comfortable when I felt suddenly cold, unusually cold. I tried to pull the duvet up, and then suddenly there was a man on my back laughing aloud. He was bearded, dirty-faced and wearing a large-collared shirt. I was terrified and struggled to get out of bed. The man appeared solid, although all I could see was his head and shoulders. The apparition lasted a couple of minutes - although I did not see it disappear. I am sure he was aware of me. I will never forget his face, or the sound of his laughter. I called my partner at work. She managed to calm me down but I never went back to bed. I made up a bed on the settee and watched television all night.

"I never saw him again, although other odd things happened in the flat, such as the hi-fi frequently switching itself on. The building, which had previously been a coach house, had been converted into flats. We later discovered that one of the builders had seen a man's ghost there during the renovation work.

"We spent ten years in our flat and every night I dreaded going to bed there. If my partner was working, I would spend nights with friends or family rather than be there alone. When we researched the history of the building, we discovered that in the 1800s it was a coach house and stables. A coachman named William Hastings had lived and worked there. Did he perhaps have a beard and a loud laugh?"

GHOST IN SLIPPERS

An elderly ghost known as 'Harry' shuffles around a house on the outskirts of Ryde, where he sits at the kitchen table in the middle of the night, opens doors, cupboards and drawers. He sets off smoke alarms and switches lights off and on too.

Meryl said that since she and her family moved into the house, off Binstead Road, in 2002, they had experienced disturbed sleep patterns and all had problems sleeping. Her eldest daughter regularly suffered nightmares between 1.30am and 3am, and often awoke screaming that there were people in her room, while her other daughter, Hailey, has seen Harry sitting on the end of her bed. Describing the ghost to her mum, she said he wore braces and horrible scruffy old patchwork carpet slippers. Since that first occasion, Harry has appeared in her room several times but this benign elderly spirit doesn't worry Hailey.

"We also have bad smells, cold spots, and every pet we have had in the house (chinchillas, budgies and a hamster) has died. Nothing seems to survive!" said Meryl.

"We can go for weeks and weeks without seeing or hearing Harry, and then without warning, he's there again. He always looks the same. He's not solid, but looks like a shadow with features. He wears old-fashioned beige-brown trousers with braces and an open waistcoat over a long-sleeved shirt. On his feet are old beige patterned carpet slippers. He's going bald, but his remaining hair is grey, flecked with white. He looks 'creased' and his face is saggy with loose folds of skin. He's about

5ft 6ins tall and appears very old; he's in his eighties or early nineties, I would say.

"Sometimes there is a 'glow' behind him. He sits in the kitchen in the early hours as though he is waiting for me. He likes to open the door to the cereal cupboard. I think he is very nosey.

"His eyes twinkle and he seems very friendly and happy, although he has never spoken. I always call out 'Hello Harry' or 'Alright Harry' when I see him there.

"He always sits in the same chair in the kitchen. He moves the chair around, and other things too, especially watches, mobile phones and keys. For some reason watches stop at 3 o'clock here.

"He's not harmful or scary; it is rather like having an elderly relative living with you. I remember there was once an old people's home here before these houses were built, so we wonder if 'Harry' was a resident there. He doesn't like change, and will disappear, sometimes for weeks at a time if we do any work here.

"When I can't sleep I often watch old black and white movies in the middle of the night. Sometimes I sense Harry is with me. It will suddenly get very cold and I just know he is sitting there watching the film, too.

"When we first saw the house, everything here was painted red, and there were black pentagrams and magical symbols on the walls in the loft. When I saw them, I didn't want to move here!

"We are used to it now, and Harry doesn't really give us much bother." Meryl added, "Since coming here we have spoken to neighbours and discovered that former residents have also reported ghosts here." (Read their story in *Most Haunted Island*)

PAVILION GHOST

The carefully preserved shell of the art nouveau Ryde Pavilion now houses the LA Bowl bowling alley, cafe, bars, amusements and the Balcony nightclub. Noise from the bowling alley fills the air, while nearby in the nightclub there's music until the early hours. But despite this, staff report the place is haunted.

This picturesque pavilion on the town's Eastern Esplanade came perilously close to destruction in 1989. After a fierce campaign by local conservationists who organised a sit-in and 5,000-name petition, it was saved at the eleventh hour and became a Grade II Listed Building.

Ryde seafront is pictured here before the Pavilion was built on the town's Eastern Gardens in 1927, at a cost of £10,025

Today the shell, with its distinctive cast ironwork and towers, remains at the centre of a busy entertainment complex, the very same purpose for which it was built by Ryde Borough in 1927 at a cost of £10,025. Since then it has served as an entertainment pavilion, theatre, nightclub and venue for many local events.

It even has an identical twin, known as the Winter Gardens at Rothesay on the Isle of Bute. This, too, was nearly demolished, but was saved and listed, to become the island's Tourist Office. It may be identical - but is it haunted - as Ryde Pavilion is?

It is not known why this 21st century entertainment complex should be haunted. Over the years however, staff at LA Bowl have noticed a number of 'odd' happenings in the old pavilion. One night when the bowling lanes were closed, several employees were standing at the bar when they heard what sounded like heavy bowling balls falling.

On checking, they found nothing was out of place. At other times the bowling lanes go down on their own. A door near the bar opens on its own, and an area behind the bar sometimes grows unnaturally cold.

Deputy manager Sam Turner said that at night, when the building is empty, a presence is felt and staff sense 'something' watching them leave.

Ryde Pavilion at the Eastern Gardens is pictured here in the 1960s

One day as a technician working in the storeroom bent to pick up a box, he saw a pair of legs standing right behind him. He spun round. No one was there. Later that day he lost a contact lens. As he hunted around in the empty room, he heard a man's low voice. "Look in the box," it said. And there inside, was the lost lens.

In the neighbouring Balcony nightclub, assistant manager Adam Goulding, who is also the maintenance and sound engineer, said, "Something is going on here too! Keys are moved, pint glasses explode and shatter on shelves, alarms are frequently triggered when the building is empty. Lights dim and flash, and sometimes as I walk away from the club, lights will start flashing when the power is turned off. When the bar is empty, heavy cast iron stools fall over by themselves."

Before the club opened one night, a former bar supervisor discovered his coat had been moved. The CCTV clearly showed him putting the coat down. Mysteriously, the system 'went blank' for ten minutes. When the picture resumed, the coat was in a different room.

"This anomaly was impossible," said Adam. "The system was still running, the cameras were all working and the battery back-up was operating. There is something rather odd going on here. We have all the systems checked regularly, but what we can't check for is a ghost."

LUSHINGTON LADY

It was the morning rush hour and traffic was heavy when Olive Lailey of Norman Way, Wootton, left her car for a service at nearby Harwood's Garage in 2007. Walking home, she went to cross the road at Lushington Hill. Although it was January, the weather was unseasonably mild. As Olive waited for a break in the traffic, she noticed an elderly lady on the pavement opposite, who also appeared to be waiting to cross the road.

"The little old lady was dressed all in black, with a long black dress and a small round hat, although she wore no coat or jacket. She stared straight ahead - which worried me because I thought she was going to step out into the traffic without looking and get run over."

As Olive watched with concern, the old lady suddenly vanished. "She disappeared right in front of my eyes. She had been standing there, right on the edge of the pavement for perhaps thirty seconds. I hadn't noticed her feet, or whether she carried anything. If I had realised she was a ghost, I would have taken more notice!

"She never seemed to see me, or the passing traffic for that matter. She appeared solid. I could see all her features but her face was blank; expressionless. She wasn't aware of the world around her. I don't know what period she came from, but it's a good job she vanished when she did, for I don't think she would ever have got across the road in one piece. Although if a car had struck the old lady, I'm sure it would have gone right through her."

Chapter Fourteen

KNIGHTON GORGES
THE ISLAND'S MOST HAUNTED HOUSE

It has been called the most haunted place on the Island, and even today the long-vanished house of Knighton Gorges seems determined to live up to its reputation. Strange things happen there still, and according to some people, what was once described as the most beautiful of the Island's ancient manors, can still be seen at certain times of the year. The haunting history of the house is told in *The Original Ghosts of the Isle of Wight* and *More Ghosts*. Anyone going ghost-hunting at Knighton Gorges, should remember the land itself is privately-owned, although the site and gateposts can be seen from the road and public footpath.

Ivor Davies fulfilled a childhood dream when he bought six acres of land on which the house once stood, and converted a seventeenth century stone barn into a holiday cottage. Since he was a boy, Knighton Gorges has held a strange fascination for Ivor, a retired consultant engineer and former Mayor of South Wight.

"It was always my dream to live there. As a boy, I would cycle out to Knighton Gorges to play there with friends. People are drawn to the place and I do understand the strange attraction which brings them."

Ivor has researched the house's history back to the Middle Ages, and has his own theories on its sudden demolition almost two centuries ago. According to local legend, it was done out of spite by Captain Maurice George Bisset, a miserly and suspicious man, who when visitors called, would withdraw to the depths of the house. It was this Captain Bisset who made the Island and two of its great mansions, Knighton Gorges and Appuldurcombe, familiar names in every London coffee house. He ran off with Seymour, the beautiful wife of Sir Richard Worsley of Appuldurcombe, and Sir Richard sued him for £20,000. The case was a sensation and neither party came out of it well. Lady Worsley admitted to having 27 lovers, and venereal disease, while Sir Richard was said to have condoned his wife's promiscuity. The jury found in Sir Richard's favour. His wife's affections had indeed been alienated. To signal their distaste they awarded him just one shilling in damages!

The mysterious, magnificent mansion of Knighton Gorges is pictured here in a rare engraving by Englefield in 1815, just six years before it was demolished

Humiliated and bitter, Maurice George Bisset returned to the Island where he was no longer welcome in fashionable circles. An exception to this was Lady Harriet Mordaunt who married Bisset after a brief courtship. They lived quietly at Knighton Gorges, producing two daughters. But Seymour had left him a parting gift – syphilis, which slowly poisoned both his body and mind. When Jane, his eldest daughter, announced her engagement to her cousin, the Reverend Fenwick, Bisset forbade the marriage. They ignored him. Bisset swore that Jane and her new husband would never set foot in the house.

Conscious that his end was near, the embittered man ordered the destruction of the house. In November 1821, an army of workmen arrived to demolish Knighton Gorges. Weeks later, it is said Maurice George Bisset died in a gardener's tiny cottage in the grounds, as the last of the timbers and stones crashed down.

Ivor holds a much less romantic but more practical theory. He thinks the upkeep of the old house had become simply too great. It had been neglected and cost too much to maintain, so Captain Bisset sold off everything he could, then ordered its demolition. By the time Bisset died on 16 December 1821, the great house was gone.

Evidence to support this theory survives just a few miles away, for the back staircase from Knighton Gorges is now in Horringford House, Arreton, while part of the main staircase graces nearby Langbridge House, Newchurch.

Stone and timber from the old manor was used in several houses built in the 1820s. So the manor of Knighton Gorges lives on.... (read the stories in *More Ghosts* and *Isle of Wight Ghosts Book Four*)

A Real Mystery Tour

Countless times in the 1950s and early '60s, local coach driver, Ted Perry of Brading, took visitors on mystery tours through Knighton Shute and Newchurch. He always stopped by the gateposts to tell passengers the tale of Knighton Gorges; how the old house had been demolished and only the gateposts, with their heraldic lions on top, had been spared.

Many people report seeing ghostly stone creatures on top of these gateposts, which stand at the entrance to the site of Knighton Gorges, pictured in 2007

This close-up of the right-hand pillar shows only the stone 'loaf of bread' sitting on top

(The coat of arms granted to Robert Dillington of Knighton Gorges in 1599 was a lion rampant)

It was a letter he wrote to the local newspaper, the Isle of Wight County Press, in 1965 that posed the riddle of the stone creatures that has intrigued people ever since. Ted took his passengers past the gateposts and stopped to tell them the story as usual. But the creatures weren't there. Thinking they had been stolen, he dashed off an angry letter to the newspaper asking if anyone knew where they were. For years afterwards controversy raged.

Many Islanders claimed to have seen the creatures, despite photographs which clearly showed the only ornamentation since the early 1900s was circular stones on top of the gateposts, known locally as 'loaves of bread'. These were a traditional sign to hungry travellers that they would be given bread and water at the kitchen door.

Ted accepted the creatures weren't there - although for years he had pointed them out to his passengers. "No one ever said a word. They either thought I was mad ... or they all saw the figures themselves," laughed Ted.

In the early 1900s, Lucy Wheeler and her husband William ran a market garden at Knighton Gardens, also renting a small piece of land which was part of the old walled kitchen garden at Knighton Gorges where they planted fruit trees.

Her granddaughter Mary Muff, said, "My mother Ivy was born there in 1899 and lived at Knighton until she started work. She knew many tales about the estate and I would listen to them in fascination. My grandmother always said there were stone animals on the gateposts. It was hard for her there after grandfather died young, at just 35. She employed an elderly widower known as 'Old Mart' to help."

Mary added, "Grandmother was once visited by a lady writer, Ethel Hargrove, who wanted to go to the site of the house to listen for the sounds of ghostly music. When news of this got around, some local Newchurch folk, including Old Mart, made sure she did hear some!"

The Spirits Emerge

Curious to see what spirits were there, retired transport manager and medium Leslie George visited Knighton Gorges one autumn afternoon in 2006.

The first presence to make contact was a young woman in her early twenties, dressed in a blue smock-type dress with a white collar, a little white silk headdress and sandals. "She came out as soon as we arrived and is happy to see visitors. She is the only one who was allowed above stairs into the main house," said Les. "I also see a young boy of ten or eleven years old. I think he was a kitchen lad. He's a rather scruffy little urchin and a cheeky one at that. Another spirit I see is a man wearing a cap, who was responsible for keeping the fires and ovens alight and supplied with wood. He chops the wood and he is showing me his axe."

Les was aware of a number of spirits who, he says, all worked in the kitchens, cellars, servants' hall, and 'below stairs' areas of the great house in different eras. "I think they died here before the place was demolished. The spirits aren't trapped but choose to remain at Knighton Gorges. It was their home and they are still happy here. Actually they have no idea of time, for whatever dimension they exist in, is timeless, and to them, the house still exists too. In our 'now', all that remains of the house are a few stones and grassy mounds, but these ghostly servants are still hard at work, keeping house at Knighton Gorges."

Many people report a strong and often violent physical reaction when they visit Knighton Gorges. Symptoms include nausea, blind panic, icy coldness, breathing difficulties, even vomiting. Cars too, have a mysterious habit of breaking down in the vicinity of Knighton Gorges.

Electrical systems cut out. Batteries are drained of energy. Many motorists refuse to drive past that lonely site after dark.

Girls With No Faces

Kellie Russell and two companions got more than they bargained for when they went looking for ghosts at Knighton Gorges, in January 2005. Her boyfriend Ben and another friend Ken were both non-believers, so she was secretly hoping something would happen to shake them up.

"We pulled up to the gates at about 12.30am and took some pictures using the flash. Every one of the photos came out black! I found this strange, as my camera never had any problems before. I returned to the car and put on the heater, as it was freezing outside. Ken decided to look around the woodland to the right of the gates. I could see him in the headlights. As Ben got back into the car, we shouted at Ken to hurry up.

"He stood with a blank expression on his face, then ran back, climbed over the fence and refused to get into the car until it was moved away from the gateposts. He was very angry with an aggressive tone to his voice."

After Ben backed out onto the road, Ken got into the car. He was shaking and was violently sick out of the window as we pulled away. When he had calmed down, he explained that he had seen little girls in dirty white pinnies - old-fashioned aprons - playing and running around the car. But these were not mortal children. They had no faces.

"This really shook us all up. Ken can be a joker, but this time we knew he wasn't messing about. We won't be going back there at night again."

The Hooded Woman

A hooded figure in a grey cloak terrified three nurses late one night, as they drove past those old gateposts. Dilys Ennion was at the wheel as the women returned home from teaching a First Aid class.

They saw a woman wearing a grey hooded cape, walking alone in the dark. Dilys stopped the car and one of the nurses got out to ask if she needed a lift.

"Suddenly she shrieked and came flying back to the car, screaming at me to drive away," said Dilys. The agitated nurse told her startled friends that the hooded woman had no face, just a grey misty emptiness where her features should have been.

Further along the road, Dilys saw a police patrol car. Flagging it down, she asked the officers to check out the mysterious figure.

Today, this grassy mound among the trees and moss-covered line of stones is all that remains of 'the most magnificent of the Island's manor houses'

"They called at our flat later that night to say they had found nothing. They laughed and told us we must have imagined it. But we all saw her and we knew it was a ghost. To this day I always lock my car doors if I have to drive along that road past Knighton Gorges," said Dilys with a shiver.

Terror on a Summer's Day

Olive Lailey knew nothing of Knighton Gorges' haunted reputation when she went hunting for dried foliage for flower arranging there, one summer's day in the 1970s. Armed with a pair of secateurs, Olive, from Norman Way, Wootton, parked by the old gateposts and walked up the drive. She soon spotted some teasels, which were just what she was looking for.

"It was a boiling hot day; everything was still and silent. Suddenly I began to feel very cold. I didn't know what was happening, but I was overcome by such a feeling of dread that I felt compelled to run back to the car and lock myself in. By now I was so cold, I was shivering and my teeth were chattering. I sat for a while wondering what the matter was. Then I drove away. I have never been back to Knighton Gorges since."

THE PHANTOM CARRIAGE

Driving home to Godshill one night in 1993, George Gray came off the Downs road into Knighton Shute. The winding road ahead was dark, but as George rounded the bend at the bottom of the hill, he slammed on the brakes. There in the road ahead was a carriage drawn by two horses, which was turning into the driveway leading to Knighton Gorges.

"It gave me quite a turn," said George. "As soon as I reached the entrance to the drive and the stone gateposts, I stopped, and looked to see where the carriage had gone. There was nothing there, and the gate was closed and padlocked. The carriage and horses, which had looked real enough in my headlights, were just ghosts from another time."

Could this be the same carriage which a local businessman saw several years earlier as he drove past Knighton Gorges, one summer night? This time the carriage, drawn by two white horses, clattered down the drive, out through the gateposts and onto the road. Then the coach and horses went straight across the road, *through* the hedge opposite, and crossed a field, disappearing into the darkness. This encounter rattled him so badly that he has not driven down that road at night since then!

Significantly, one of the few known engravings of Knighton Gorges in Worsley's 1781 History of the Isle of Wight shows a track - which no longer exists - running across this very field. (See picture on next page)

SECRETS OF THE PAST

It is almost two centuries since the old house was pulled down and yet to the spirits that live on there, existing in their own dimension, mortal time has ceased to matter.

Do we, the eager ghost-hunters appear to them as insubstantial spirits. Do they view us as ungodly intruders? We arrive in our horseless carriages, dressed in strange modern attire, armed with what must appear to them as sinister devices like cameras, camcorders and sound recording equipment. Do they resent our presence? Apparently they do for Chris, a medium, who visited Knighton Gorges in April 2006, was

This engraving from Worsley's History shows Knighton Gorges from the road

immediately targeted by a belligerent spirit as he walked through those stone gateposts.

"He was upon me immediately," Chris said. "He didn't want me here, and as I was looking across the site, I felt a sharp push which sent me straight into a barbed wire fence, ripping my shirt. The meaning was clear. Keep out. This place is mine!"

However, with the permission of owner Ivor Davies, Chris spent two hours recording his impressions of what he confirms is a very active and haunted place.

He reported, "There are a number of different spirits here. One man connected with Knighton Gorges was tried and hung for treason. There are Royal links, and there has been a small battle or fight somewhere in the grounds. There was once a chapel on the site and bodies are buried here in ancient graves. (It was reported in 1905 that human bones had been dug up on the property).

"Horse-drawn carriages still clatter down the driveway to the front of the house. Three ladies died here over the centuries - one by suffocation, one by a knife, and the third of old age. The names Christina and Mary are connected, and the dates 1729 and 1762 are significant. There is also a woman with a 'P' name, a nice, gentle lady who died here in 1592. She is still around.

"There is a deep well on the site and the spirit of a little girl who died of an illness can be seen near it. A young man named Daniel worked with horses here. His life was cut short after he fell in love with a daughter of the house. Bad things were done to him before he died."

Venting his malice

"The overwhelming presence at Knighton Gorges however, is that of a middle-aged man who radiates anger and resentment, venting his malice on visitors to what he still considers is 'HIS' home. His limbs shake as he trembles with palsy, his complexion is florid, he suffers from gout, shortness of breath and has tightness around the throat. He has a very low opinion of ladies and holds them in contempt. He will often target females when they come here, sucking energy from them, attacking their psychic defences so they feel dizzy, faint and sick. He projects himself onto them and thoroughly enjoys their reactions. He is the one drawing energy from visitors and from their vehicles. He is responsible for the power drains that so many people experience here. He moves freely around his old estate and also shows himself on the road outside. I feel April 19th is an important date, and I think he lived here during the 18th or 19th century. His health was poor, his temper short, and he was not a nice man to be around when he was alive. Now he has passed on, he is exactly the same. He resents visitors and simply doesn't want us here. He is aware that he is dead, but won't move on. His attachment to Knighton Gorges - transcending the boundaries of time and death - is just too strong."

Does this describe the bitter man that Maurice George Bisset became in the years following the scandal of the Worsley trial? Returning to Knighton Gorges, ridiculed and shunned by society, his mind and his body slowly poisoned by syphilis - Seymour Worsley's final gift to him - this man would finally destroy the magnificent home he loved to spite his daughter and deny her inheritance.

Is the malignant passion of Maurice George Bisset so strong that it lives on … where a ruined gateway leads to a haunted hill that still goes by the name of Knighton Gorges?

THE END

THE AUTHOR

Thousands of ghosts, spirits and apparitions, haunt the Isle of Wight, the world's most haunted island. Powerful unseen energy or 'ley' lines run under this British island, just 70 miles from London, which attracts ghost-hunters, paranormal researchers and enthusiasts from around the world.

Gay Baldwin started researching and recording ghost stories here in 1977, when the first book, *Ghosts of the Isle of Wight*, written with Ray Anker was published. There's no shortage of hauntings on Ghost Island. *More Ghosts, Ghosts of the Isle of Wight III, Isle of Wight Ghosts Book 4, Ghost Island* and *Most Haunted Island* have also been best sellers.

Gay also devised the popular Ghost Island walks, a series of historical walks with a supernatural slant, which have introduced thousands of Islanders and visitors to the darker side of places such as Newport, Cowes, Arreton, Appuldurcombe, Niton and Ventnor Botanic Gardens. For more information visit: *www.ghost-tours.co.uk*

Although not particularly psychic herself, as a journalist and a member of the Ghost Club Society and patron of several other paranormal research groups, Gay has met and interviewed many hundreds of people who have incredible and inexplicable stories of hauntings to tell. She then researches the history of the sites or houses involved, looking for reasons behind the ghostly happenings. Some accounts defy rational explanation and this seventh book of Isle of Wight ghost stories will give the most confirmed sceptic pause for thought.

Some of the things that go bump in the night are easily explained away. An over-active imagination can conjure up all sorts of 'ghostly' sounds, smells and apparitions. Creaking timbers; skeletal branches tap tapping on window panes; owls or bats in flight after dark; mice or rats scurrying through attics or behind walls, can be the innocent origin of many a ghost story. But not in every case...

After more than thirty years of writing about ghosts, Gay firmly believes in the world of spirit and the supernatural. Too many people; reasonable, rational, sensible people; have had experiences and encounters which cannot be explained away by anything other than the supernatural.

Gay would like to hear any strange tales of ghosts or hauntings that you might have. You can ring her on 01983 294651 or e-mail: *gb@hauntediw.demon.co.uk*

You can also check her website at *www.ghostisland.com* for news, photographs and more stories from the World's Most Haunted Island.

BIBLIOGRAPHY

AND FURTHER READING

Kokeritz, Helge - The Place-names of the Isle of Wight.
Eldridge, R.J. - Newport in Bygone Days.
Davenport-Adams, W.H. – The Isle of Wight, 1888
By-laws of the House of Industry, 1838
Hassell - Tour of the Isle of Wight.
Bullar, John - Guide to the Isle of Wight, 1821.
Cooke's Isle of Wight, 1813.
Winter, C.W.R. - This Enchanted Isle.
Cox, J.Charles - Country Churches of the Isle of Wight.
Albin - Companian or Vectiana, 1806.
Mitchell, Kevin - Newport Pubs
Searle, Adrian - Isle of Wight at War
Mudie's Hampshire.
Jones, Jack and Johanna - The Isle of Wight,
An Illustrated History.
Garle, Hubert - A Driving Tour of the Isle of Wight.
Shepard, Bill - Newport Remembered.
Underwood, Peter - Ghosts and How to See Them.
Worsley, Richard - A History of the Isle of Wight, 1781.
J.W. Hill and Co, IW Directory, 1871.
John Matson – Dear Osborne, 1878
Laidlaw, Eric – A History of Isle of Wight Hospitals, 1994
Ethel C Hargrove – Wanderings in the Isle of Wight 1913
Niton Women's Institute – Niton Calling, 1971
Brighstone Village

NOT SPOOKED YET?

WHY NOT ORDER YOUR SIGNED COPIES OF THE OTHER BOOKS, AUDIOBOOKS, MAP AND DVD IN THIS SERIES?

Photocopy or send this order form to:

Gay Baldwin, 9 Pine Tree Close, Cowes, Isle of Wight PO31 8DX
Telephone: 01983 294651   e-mail: *gb@hauntediw.demon.co.uk*

Original Ghosts of the Isle of Wight	@ £4.95	£..............
More Ghosts *(book two)*	@ £5.95	£..............
Ghosts of the Isle of Wight *(book three)*	@ £6.95	£..............
Isle of Wight Ghosts *(book four)*	@ £6.95	£..............
Ghost Island *(book five)*	@ £7.95	£..............
Most Haunted Island *(book six)*	@ £8.95	£..............
Even More Ghosts *(book seven)*	@ £8.95	£..............
Ghost Island DVD	@ £12.95	£..............
Osborne House CD audiobook	@ £8.95	£..............
Knighton Gorges CD audiobook	@ £8.95	£..............
The Isle of Wight Ghost Hunter's Map	@ £1.00	£..............

Just add £1.00 postage and packing for each book and DVD (eg 2 books & 1 DVD=£3.00 postage) for CD audiobooks and maps add 30p each   **Postage**   £..............

TOTAL   £..............

Please make cheque/postal order payable to: Gay Baldwin.

NOTE: I usually dispatch orders the same or next day. Please allow two weeks before you panic. Let me know if you would like your books signed.

You can also order on-line at *www.ghost-island.com*

Name ....

Address ....

.... Post Code ....

Telephone .... e-mail ....